YOU
Make a Difference

YOU
Make a Difference

27 Amazing Young People and Their Advocates Share Their Stories of Inspiration and Transformation

Featuring stories by:

Keb' Mo', Four-time Grammy Award Winning Blues Musician

Jesse James Leija, Two-time Boxer World Champion

Judge Laura Parker, Baxter County Judge

Senator Leticia Van de Putte, Texas State Senate, District 26

Jackie Van De Walle, Community Leader and Past President of Van De Walle Industries, Inc.

LEON SMITH
PUBLISHING

ISBN: 978-1-945446-41-2

This book is dedicated to the
One in Five Minds organization and the
incredible children they serve.

Contents

AMAZING
YOUNG PEOPLE

ADVOCATES

Acknowledgments

The publishers would like to thank the following people:

Kathy Wells, Manny Goldman, Gerard Migeon, Rebecca Helterbrand, Judge Laura Parker, Jackie Van De Walle, Keb' Mo', Alyssa Narro, Lee Nichols, Jesse James Leija, Mike Hanna, Larry Mills, Lissa Coffey, Pamela Parish, Bruce Dickson, Kip Brooks, Mark Wells, Linda M. Stephens, CK Brown, Michelle Taufmann, Randy and Lisa Collins, Lisa Drennan, David Boufford, Bradlee Snow, George Huang, and all the children and teenagers who submitted their answers for inclusion in this book.

Introduction

A number of years ago, we did the first *You Make a Difference* book, which featured heart-centered entrepreneurs sharing their stories of inspiration and transformation. The book turned out great, and we wanted to do another one.

So, we asked ourselves: *What group of people would we like to feature this time?*

We always enjoyed speaking with teens and sharing with them the things we wish had been shared with us as teens.

Things like:

- Bullies are bullies because they're bullied at home.

- Life is like a rollercoaster. You are whipped around; you go down; you are whipped around again. If you hang in there, you'll always go up again.

- You make a profound difference every day whether you realize it or not. Without even trying, you're touching lives everywhere you go.

We set out to create a book to help teens realize how much of a difference they make. While sharing the book project idea with one of our authors, Kat Wells, we discovered not only did Kat share our desire to work with teens, she also knew of an organization supporting young people in dealing with the feelings and issues we had in mind. The organization, Clarity Child Guidance Center, sponsors a campaign called *One in Five Minds*. When we looked at their website, we saw these people were doing amazing work, and we quickly realized this book would not only inspire teens but could support the *One in Five Minds* campaign as an educational and fund-raising tool.

On the website (1in5minds.org), we learned that one in five children suffers from mental, emotional, or behavioral problems, and only one in five of those children actually receives treatment.

When children do not receive help:

- Half of them drop out of high school.

- They are twice as likely to start using drugs and alcohol.

- They are more likely to end up in the juvenile system.

- Many attempt suicide.

In the first *You Make a Difference* book, we came up with a series of questions to ask each of the featured entrepreneurs why they do what they do, how they get through the hard times, and what miracles they had witnessed through their work that would inspire other entrepreneurs to start or keep moving forward. For this new edition of the book series, we wanted teens to share about who had made a difference in their lives, and we also wanted them to reach out and ask the people in their families and schools how they had made a difference in those people's lives. Finally, we wanted to find out what change they want to see in the world, and what part they see themselves playing in bringing about that change.

Next, we found out about some incredible and influential adults who were also supporters of young people in the *One in Five Minds* campaign. When we asked them the same questions we asked the teens, their answers were equally inspirational.

Hearing the answers to these questions was inspiring to us and made a difference in our lives. We hope that it will make a difference in yours.

To find out more about the *One in Five Minds* campaign, go to: www.1in5minds.org

Amazing
Young People

Caitlyn Bradley

Grade: 10

Hobbies: I like to write, swim, and hang out with my friends.

What do you do for fun? I write, watch anime, hang out with friends, listen to music, watch movies, and play games.

Favorite class: Japanese

What would you like to be, or do, once you've completed school? I'm going to become an OBGYN when I get out of college, but I also plan to have a writing career on the side.

1. Who has made the greatest difference in your life, and what did they do?

Some people I used to hang out with in sixth grade made the biggest impact in my life. They were my friends at first, and then they bullied me, really bad.

Tara, Rebecca, and I were *the trio* in sixth grade: the greatest friends ever. We found out that our names spelled

CTR; it was really awesome. I was enjoying the friendship, but there was always growing conflict. Whenever I paid attention to one friend, the other friend was kind of ignored. It was hard to hang out with more than just one person because it's hard to pay attention to two people at once. That's what I learned from that.

We were really tight in sixth grade, and there were three different classes in my elementary school that I used to go to. We used to do rotations for sixth grade science — one teacher taught the moon phases, another teacher taught about space, and another taught mostly biology. The teacher I had taught about biology most of the days — mold and stuff; it was fun.

I remember one day when I came back to my desk after the science rotation, I found a note. My friends and I thought it was always fun to leave notes on each other's desks; because we were so close, we wanted to let each other know that we were sitting in each other's desks. We didn't all share the same class — we had different teachers — so it was really easy to do that. I remember finding that note in my desk. I took it out of my desk and started reading it. I'm pretty sure this was after lunch too. I started reading it, and it started out nice. I thought: *Oh, it's from my friend!* Then it got worse and worse, and they started calling me bad names, saying that I was a piece of crap and I didn't deserve to be friends with anyone. They said I'd never be popular, never make it in the world, and should just go away. That's what my first friend said.

I won't say who wrote which because I don't think that's fair, but my first friend wrote a lot of swear words in it. I know that my mom kept the note somewhere around here, but I don't know where it is so I can't share it. My second friend wrote a simple one. My first friend took up most of the page; my second friend only took up a paragraph of the page. She wrote in simple letters that she didn't want to be friends with me because I was childish, and I couldn't be cool. That's what they were doing.

I remember my teacher, Mrs. Cooper, took me out into the hallway and asked me why I was crying. I handed her the note. She seemed disappointed in the people who did that to me, but she couldn't really do anything about it. I went home that day and showed my mom, and she was very disappointed too. That's why she kept the note because it was really bad. After that, I had a really hard time even looking at them, and I know they were banned from ever sitting at my desk again because they could possibly keep putting notes in there and harassing me. I know they turned some people away from me. I lost a lot of friends that year and a lot of respect because they spread rumors about me. I had a really hard year, but Mrs. Cooper really helped me through sixth grade. I always played sick, wanting to come home because I didn't want to face the school day.

In elementary school, you had to have good grades to be on student council, and after going into a little depression, I threw myself into school work. The student council member from our class had moved, and she chose me because it had to be a boy and a girl. She was one of my friends, so it was hard that she moved away, but I became the student council member. I got to go bowling and all of that stuff; it was really fun!

The friend who really helped me the most through my sixth-grade elementary school experience was my friend, Colton. He was really nice and we played superheroes. It's kind of childish for that age, but I know I was in a deep depression up until ninth grade because of that experience.

I tried becoming friends with those girls again, and we were friends for maybe a couple of months. But one of the friends called me saying they didn't want to be friends with me anymore over the phone, breaking my little heart once again. They really hurt me throughout my life. We became friends after that again, but certain things happened and we're not friends anymore. We're acquaintances.

I know that during those years I was depressed; I really wanted to commit suicide. I remember walking into my dad's room to go get a video cassette, because we still owned those (they're so old fashioned, wow!). I don't know if prescription drugs were on the same *thing* as the VCR, but I remember seeing prescription stuff on there. I remember thinking that I could take any of those and probably die, and I'd be fine. My father also owns a lot of guns, but he keeps the guns [in a] safe so I obviously wouldn't have gotten into it. But I thought I could have gotten into the gun safe somehow and shot myself.

During those years, I thought of suicide a lot. I was very depressed, and I think I forgot how to smile.

I had started writing in seventh grade, and I showed my aunt my fun story. It was supposed to be a serious story, but when I look at it now, it's kind of funny because it's based off a few *animes* that I thought were awesome. My aunt was telling me about my cousin, Elizabeth, and how she was a good writer and loved to write with people. Elizabeth then messaged me over Facebook, telling me that she was interested in writing with me because my aunt had recommended me, and I had a really big imagination — which I still do — and she'd like to write with me if I wanted to. I said sure, and she told me all the rules: You can't control the character that the other person made. Just have fun. If you don't have powers, your character can't just suddenly have powers. You have to stick to the same type of storyline; if it started off as sci-fi, it had to stay sci-fi — it couldn't suddenly turn out to be fantasy. Those were the rules of the game.

We started writing, and I know that I started getting a little bit happier. I remember smiling a little bit more. I was always so happy and excited when she messaged me back! I know that I was probably sounding very childish when I was writing. That was two years ago, which made me around thirteen or fourteen. I didn't know how to use punctuation like periods, commas, paragraphs, and stuff like that. It would just be this glob of a part, but she helped teach me. She learned a little bit of how I write, then I learned a lot from her with how she wrote. I know how to form paragraphs and stuff like that.

We didn't write a lot during the first story that we did together, but then we started getting more into it when we were writing the second story. It was really awesome and fun. I remember smiling and being a little bit happier. I didn't think of suicide a lot after that, but I know it went through my mind because negative thoughts are addicting to the human mind. I was taking in those negative thoughts, and those negative thoughts kept coming back. It was like I was on drugs of negative thoughts because that always happened. My recommendation to that was to think more positively.

I just know that I smiled a lot more after I started writing. I used to think I was a good singer, but when I went into seventh grade and took choir, I found out that I wasn't the best. That put me down too. In ninth grade, I was lifted up more when I took seminary, and I also had another friend, Kristen, who is really awesome and helped pull me out of it completely. I know I wasn't totally out of it during ninth grade, but I know halfway through ninth grade I just popped out, and I was suddenly so happy and outgoing. I know during the years of seventh and eighth grade I wasn't a very good student. I promised my mom I would try harder in ninth grade, and I got As everywhere. I thought: *Oh yeah, I can do this!*, and I became happier.

2. In whose life have you made the greatest difference, and what did you do?

I talked to three people: my mom, my cousin Elizabeth, and my friend Kristen about this. I'm going to talk to you about my mom first. My mom is Tambria Bradley, and she is the best mom I've ever had, probably because she's the only one!

I remember sitting down in front of her; she looked at me, she smiled, and said, "You are my first daughter, out of four boys, and you have helped teach me many things. You help make my day feel brighter. You make me smile a lot, and I'm just very grateful that you are in my life. You are a very big helper, and I would not have forgiven you if you had committed suicide." (I told her about that time).

My mom said I helped her through a lot. She said that I have the warmest hugs in the family because whenever she starts to cry, I come up to her and I just hug her and hold her. She knows the love I have for her as her daughter.

Elizabeth said that I helped her a lot with her wedding. She's very grateful that I was there to help. I always made her smile even though she was feeling a lot of stress and opposition throughout her engagement with her husband-to-be (who is now her husband). She was very grateful that I was there and cheered up her day with my writing and how I write. I love to make people smile because I know how it feels not to smile, and it pains me when I know that my friends are down. I think: *Hey, I can help you!*

Elizabeth also said that my writing has gotten a lot better; it's almost professional level. I don't see it because I still need to make everything flow, but I'll work on that later. I know that she said that she was very grateful I was in her life and that my aunt told us to write together. She knows that she probably wouldn't be the same without me in her life.

There was a Doctor Who quote on Facebook. There were two pictures, and the top one said that there are seven billion people in this world. The quote: "I'm just one person, they don't need me." And in the second picture, it shows the Tardis and the Doctor Who quote: "In my nine-hundred and some-odd years, I have never met someone who wasn't important." That's what Elizabeth sent to me, and she said I really made a big impact on her life and that she loves me a lot. She has said she loves me a lot ever since that time because I guess she felt that I was down and I really needed to get this question answered.

My friend Kristen has been through a lot in the last year. She is so pretty and beautiful. She has the most amazing eyes; they're almost black, but in the sun, they're a nice brown. I remember when she told me she was adopted.

I asked her, "You're adopted?"

She said, "Yeah, I'm from Bulgaria."

I then said, "That's the coolest thing I've heard — *ever!*" I'd never met someone who was adopted. She said when she first met me, I looked like a loner. I pretty much was because I didn't have any friends. She came up to me, started talking to me, and never expected what happened between us to grow. But, we are like sisters now. We met at the beginning of ninth grade in P.E.

She said that when her grandfather died last year in March, she was going through a really hard time. She was kind of depressed and didn't know what to do with herself. She felt like everyone was mad at her except me. She felt like I understood her, even though I don't really know the pain of losing a grandfather. Her grandfather was like a father to her, and I don't know what it's like losing a father. She said that she was starting to lose hope in her religion and felt that God wasn't there for her.

She always came to me, and when I talked to her, she said it was like I was glowing and I had all this faith, and that I believed in her. It really helped her throughout that. I don't know if she's gotten over her grandfather's death; I know she misses him a lot. I met him a few times, and he seemed like a very, very nice person. I remember he tried to make jokes; he was very funny. She told me that she wouldn't be a member of our church, the Church of Jesus Christ of Latter-Day Saints. The Church of LDS is what people call Mormons, but really it's the LDS Church. But she said that she wouldn't be a Mormon anymore if I hadn't helped her through it.

3. What difference would you like to see in the world, and what are you willing to do to contribute to it?

I know that being a doctor means I can save lives and all that stuff, but I really want to be a writer badly because I know that my writing can be inspirational and funny. I don't want anyone to go through the same things that I did because it really hurts a lot. I don't know what it feels like for someone close to me to commit suicide, but I know it's hard. One of my friend's friends did, and she was just down. I want to help save people from making that mistake. I want to make people smile; that's my goal every day. I remember at seminary one time, they asked me: *If you could do something different yesterday, what would it be?* I said I would give more people hugs and smile at more people. I'd try to get to know more people and make them feel better about themselves.

The reason I want to be an OBGYN doctor is because I can bring newborn babies into the world. I can help teenage girls who get pregnant, throughout their pregnancy. But I'd rather be a writer because I know that I can probably inspire lives. I just need the right push to get into that career, to help people, because I love to help people. It's in my blood to help people, and it's part of my religion, that service. Whenever I see a sad person, I just want to give them a hug, but I know it would be awkward for them. I try talking to them, but they usually ignore me, which is sad.

I know there's a quote somewhere that says: *I want to make a difference in the world so I'll leave this mark to what I did.*

That is what I want to do. I want to write to let people know they're not the only ones going through the same thing I did or other things.

Do you know what an empath is? They feel people's emotions. Abraham Lincoln was one; that's why he freed the slaves. I learned that a few years ago. I know I'm one of those, and I can't help but feel other people's pain. I want to help them because in my heart, I know they don't deserve to go through it because they're a child of God. They can get through this if only they'll let someone help them.

Humans can be very prideful, and they won't ask for help even if they're going through a trial that is harder than they can handle. The difference I want to make is: I want to make the world record for the most hugs to ever be given to people. It's kind of weird, but I just know that there are a lot of people on this Earth; I just want to hug every single one of them and tell them what they're going through is just a trial of their faith and they can get through it. They just need to hold on, and they shouldn't make the decision to commit suicide. I think every two hours someone commits suicide. When I heard that, my heart broke and I thought: *I don't want that to happen, ever.*

I think I would make a bigger difference if I were a writer than a doctor because some people love to read.

I know you're probably going to find me weird, but I hate reading! That's probably why I wouldn't be a good editor. I just write; that's all I do. It takes a really, really good hook for me to start reading something. The book *Eon* just fascinated me. It was about ancient China, and I just fell in love with it so I was able to read it. It was five hundred pages; it was a thick book. But I read it all, and I wanted to read more of that series. There were two books, and the second one had six hundred and some-odd pages, and I read all of it. I know that if I were a writer, I could inspire more people because it would spread all the way out to China or Japan. I know being a doctor could inspire people, but not as well as a writer. I just need that push to become a popular writer. I know I can do it. I just need help because I can't do it by myself.

David Clubb

Grade: 11

Hobbies: Singing, dancing, and volunteering

What do you do for fun? Hang out with my friends, sing and dance

Favorite class: U.S. History

What would you like to be, or do, once you've completed school? I'd like to be a professional singer.

1. Who has made the greatest difference in your life, and what did they do?

For me, there are two people. One would be my step-dad—but to me, he's really just my dad, Sam, because he took full responsibility for me. He treated me like I was his own son. He cared for me like I was his own son. He didn't have to do that. I've heard of other relationships with people's stepfathers where there's not a real relationship there, where they're not friends or anything like that. Sam has really become one of my best friends. Even through all the struggles and all the arguments, it's really nice at the end of the day to know we're angry with each other because of how much we love each other. He's worried about me and just wants the best for me, and I'm just being the typical teenage son who always has a problem with their dad.

To know that relationship is there means a lot. He's really taught me how to be a man, how to live life, and who I want to be as a person. He's taught me a lot. Also, it's great to have somebody who just really gets you and can understand the different connection. We're not there by blood, but we're there by love, and that's what made us family. I love him so much.

Then there is another one—my youth pastor, Josh. I've only known him for about a year, and he's become my mentor and my best friend. If there's a problem between me and Sam, I can go to Josh, and Josh will help me to understand where he's coming from so I look at it from a different angle, like I'm looking at it as a third party. I'm in the conflict, and he shows me from the outside view what's really going on.

It's funny. Even if I'm angry and I'm telling Josh about what's going on, he can still sit there and say, "Okay, now what did you do?" It's really funny when he asks me that question because I'm in my anger thinking: *Well I did nothing to him!* I end up sitting there realizing: *Actually, here is what I did.* He'll help me apologize and be able to come back to my dad so that I can understand what I did in the scenario too.

2. In whose life have you made the greatest difference, and what did you do?

This is kind of a wild story. There's a friend of mine at my church. When I first started going, we didn't get along. We weren't very friendly towards each other, and that was because I was still a newborn Christian. I didn't exactly believe in the ideals yet, and I didn't understand things. As I grew, our friendship grew, and now we're like brothers!

We lead a middle school small group together. He got so comfortable with me, that he finally came out and talked about how he was feeling. No one knew; we all thought he was okay. We all thought everything was fine with him, but when he told me all the things, he was saying his family life at home was always a struggle. His parents were always arguing, he and his dad were always arguing, and there was never really a family connection there anymore. His mom and dad were probably going to get a divorce, and he was struggling and having a hard time.

When he told me all of this, originally he sent me this message through text. He talked about his family and the fact he was bisexual and felt so uncomfortable with being that. He thought there was something wrong with him because he was this way. He thought: *I shouldn't feel this way; I should only like girls.*

Because I knew I was going to see him the next day, I told him: *I'm not going to talk about this with you through text.*

I waited until the next day to talk to him in person, and we sat down to talk. I think we went out to lunch or something. I said to him, "First of all, there is nothing wrong with you. Just because you like both genders doesn't mean anything; you're still you. That is just a part of who you are, and if you're so worried that your friends aren't going to accept you for that, then they're not your friends. Those people are not your friends. You know in our family church, you can tell us anything, and we're still going to love you through it."

He then told me he was cutting himself. I was so worried about him after we had this first part of the conversation, that when we got to the subject of his parents, I said, "Look, at the end of the day, your parents love you no matter what. You may think that your parents don't love you; you may think that your parents don't love each other. Your parents love each other. Now, there might be a different standpoint to how they love each other because of the problems that are going on, but at the end of the day, they still love each other and they love you. Just because they're arguing doesn't affect how much they love you. Your family loves you, and no matter what you think or say, they're always going to love you. If they don't, that would be ridiculous, because they do. They're your family. There's that unspoken love that's already there when you're born, and nothing's going to change that. No matter what happens, they're still your family, and you're going to have a great relationship with all of them."

When he told me about the cutting. I told him, "If it makes you feel any better, when I was in eighth grade, I was going through a lot of problems. The drama at school was bad, and I got to the point where I was doing that too. All I wanted to do was just end my life, but I didn't. There was something at the end of the day that kept getting me through. Originally and honestly, that *latch* I was holding onto was my sister. That was the one thing; she needed an older brother. She needed me, and I needed her. She looked up to me. How selfish would I be to leave? I'm not just saying find one thing and hold onto it, but find several things because you know you can call me any time you want. You can always talk to me, no matter what time it is or anything like that. If I'm asleep, I'll text you as soon as I wake up."

A couple of weeks ago, he came back, and he came out to a lot of the people at our church, in our little Houston family. He told them about himself and said he was no longer uncomfortable with who he was. He took what I said about his family to heart, and he learned that, even if he was arguing with his dad, at the end of an argument he would make sure he came back later to say, "Dad, I love you." He's starting to feel a little bit better about himself.

3. What difference would you like to see in the world, and what are you willing to do to contribute to it?

This is a hard one! I don't like seeing all this violence in the world over the resources that we *need*. Why aren't we all coming together to try and fix this? Why are we always fighting over these resources?

I'm sure there's something where, if we really took the time, we could sit down and actually find a way to get through this. Yes, I know — according to what the mass media sends out — that we have to *fight the terrorists,* but why? The terrorists are there in response to things that we do. I'm not saying I'm with them, but why are we saying what we do is any better? We're going into other countries, we're taking things that we want, and we're just leaving them. Yes, we've done a couple of good things along the way, but we're not really contributing anything.

We're starting to hurt the environment more than we're helping it. We're focusing on little things, but we're not focusing on the big things. There is stuff in this world that we're losing; we've been in a drought for, what, a couple of years now? We need to start worrying about the environment more than we're worrying about silly, petty little fights. Without this earth, we're not going to be able to go anywhere.

I'm willing to share my beliefs with anybody who will listen, but at the same time, I try to — environmental-wise — take shorter showers. When I brush my teeth,

I try not to have the water running. When I'm shaving, I only leave the water on so that I can rinse the shaver out, then I turn it back off. I make sure that if I see trash on the street, I pick it up so that it doesn't go into our ocean. At my school, my geo-science teacher had us do waste characterization charts. These two people would bring in trash that they would find on the beaches and stuff; they would rinse them or wash them, then bring them to our class to characterize it. These were just going into the ocean, and I looked at what washes up. It's ridiculous how much is there!

It's kind of sad. I just want the world to change. I want it to be better. I don't like war. I wish we could end war and just focus on environmental stuff and relationships. We can be one people. We *are* one people, so why are we going off and killing others?

Diana Todisco

Grade: Senior in college

Hobbies: Horseback riding, skiing, swimming, Facebook, dancing, singing, and playing the guitar

What do you do for fun? All the above

Favorite class: Anything to do with my major, Public Communications

What would you like to be, or do, once you've completed school? A film editor

1. Who has made the greatest difference in your life, and what did they do?

My wonderful Italian grandmother's voice still echoes in my head saying: *Que sera sera, whatever will be will be.* She had this infectious smile and loving personality. She could always make you feel better and cook something amazing. She reminds me every day to take things day by day, and that she is always looking out for me.

2. In whose life have you made the greatest difference, and what did you do?

I think that the greatest difference I've made is in my parent's lives. I am my dad's first daughter and my mom's first child. I know that they have learned how to be amazing parents, and I'd like to think I had something to do with the people who they have become.

3. What difference would you like to see in the world, and what are you willing to do to contribute to it?

There are so many changes I'd like to see in the world. I wish that there was no more violence or war, that we would take care of our planet and really start to fix the problems we have created. I would like to contribute by spreading awareness and really trying to get that impact across to people to change their behavior to be healthier, more sustainable, and better for the world.

Emily Rice

Grade: 12

What do you do for fun? I like to watch TV.

Favorite class: My favorite class is Anatomy. It's a college course, so it's pretty hard, but I love doing doctor stuff.

What would you like to be, or do, once you've completed school? I'd like to travel the world.

1. Who has made the greatest difference in your life, and what did they do?

I think everyone makes a difference in my life to some extent. Probably the people who are closest to me, like my family and friends, make the biggest difference.

There was a time when I had back problems and my whole leg would go numb. I ended up having surgery because of this. After the surgery, I felt scared and alone. I didn't have many people around to console me because I don't really let people in. My mother was there for me after the surgery. I had to stay in bed to heal, and it was great to have Mom there with me. I would put my hand out, and she would hold it for what seemed like hours. I feel like this brought us closer together. Since the surgery, I feel like we really talk about things more, instead of just yelling at each other and storming off. I've learned to trust her more, and I realize that she really cares about me. This makes me feel good.

Also after my surgery, my brother would watch the movie *Frozen* with me. It was the only movie we agreed on. I can quote every word and song of the movie. It was great to have this time with him, and I realized that he, too, cared about me. He was helping to take care of me while I healed. I am the older sister, so really it's my job to take care of him, but there he was, sitting by my side, watching my favorite movie with me. It meant a lot to me.

2. In whose life have you made the greatest difference, and what did you do?

I have a friend who is going through a really hard time. In my opinion, she's doing way too many drugs and drinking too much alcohol. It feels to me like she's becoming an addict. She's dealing with a lot of emotions and emotional things in her life, and she doesn't know how to get past them. I worry about her.

The way I feel I've impacted her life is by always being there for her and letting her know that I think she's important. I think that if you're going through tough times, usually you'll meet someone in your life that's going through a tough time too, and you'll bond over it. Maybe you won't be going through exactly the same things, but close enough you can relate to each other and share things to help each other. This helps people to bond. This is what happened with my friend and me, and I know it's brought us closer together.

One example was when I was in the healing process from my surgery. I was feeling alone, and she was going through some emotional problems at that time. We helped each other through the stuff. It's not really about the problems we were dealing with, but it was about our holding each other up during those times that seemed so hard. It has brought us together as friends. We don't judge each other; we just help each other.

I've known her for years now, and we've really been through some things. She had tried to kill herself before, but I wanted to talk about her second attempt. When I heard that she had tried to kill herself, I was so upset that I couldn't go to school. I didn't even feel like leaving the house. I had like a mental breakdown over it. When I finally saw her, I told her, "I was the most worried about you ever. It scared me, and I really had a breakdown over it."

When she heard this, she said, "Thank you so much. That really means a lot to me."

There was another time when she came to school drunk, and she thought that getting in a trashcan would be kind of funny. She climbed in the can, but there was gum in the trashcan — so it stuck to her. I helped her get out of the can and to get the gum off her before anyone in our class saw it. It would have been embarrassing for her, and I didn't want that. I think friendship is about being there for each other in times like these.

3. What difference would you like to see in the world, and what are you willing to do to contribute to it?

I would like to see schools serve food that's worth eating. They serve food that has no nutritional value to us and act like it's good for us. That upsets me. If it were up to me, there would be more healthy options. There would be a salad bar, and in the section that has pizza and spaghetti, there would be more nutritious options. We can't eat all starches, pasta, and dairy products and expect to be healthy. I think we should add more fruits and vegetables and cut back on the fried foods.

If I were brave, I would go to the school board and try to get this changed. They actually have tons of frozen foods in the freezer at our school. These will last for years, but they aren't good for us. I think the first sign of foods that are worth eating is they are fresh foods. Foods not able to be frozen, fresh foods — these are the ones worth eating, in my opinion.

How about if schools struck some type of deal with the markets and got them to deliver fresh and healthy foods? That would be good.

Jamie Oliver went into some schools and tried to change the meal plan, but it didn't really work. Jamie said, "Imagine a world where children were fed tasty and nutritious, real food at school from the age of four to eighteen: a world where every child was educated about how amazing food is, where it comes from, how it affects the body, and how it can save their lives." I'd like to work with him and help him get foods in the school systems changed.

Last year, I wrote a paper about getting healthy foods into our schools. Maybe I could edit the article I wrote and submit it to the school board. Also, I could look at his website, find his contact info, and send the article to him. This would be a great first step to making a difference.

I have one idea of what a healthy cafeteria would look like.

At my school, we have a big cafeteria and I think it can be divided into five sections:

- A home cooked meal section (warm, healthy comfort foods)

- A salad bar (It's always fresh veggies and changes daily.)

- A vegetarian section (Yes, there are some vegetarians at my school.)

- A fresh sandwich section where we can build our own healthy sandwiches

- A smoothie section (Athletes can add extra protein into their smoothies.)

Also, many students would like to be chefs when they grow up, so we could offer a class for those students. They could get class credits and life experience by setting up these different sections, serving, and cleaning up. They could rotate sections and learn about each section in the process. One day, they learn about home cooked meals, the next day about the vegetarian foods, another day about sandwiches, and smoothies the next day. For those who want to go into this after school, it would help them get real life experience in something they have an interest in. It would become a teaching thing and help students in school get to eat healthy foods. Seems like a good plan to me.

Hannah Maddux

Grade: 7

Hobbies: I like volleyball and tennis, and I play the saxophone.

What do you do for fun? Hang out with my friends and with my cousin. I like to swim and jump on the trampoline.

Favorite class: Science — I have a 100 percent average in science.

What would you like to be, or do, once you've completed school? I'd want to go to Texas A&M University and major in veterinarian science to be a veterinarian. I want to focus on exotic animals, as well as the usual animals. It would be interesting to learn to help exotic animals.

1. Who has made the greatest difference in your life, and what did they do?

That's a good question!

I would have to say my mom has made a really great difference in my life, and so has my dad — I mean, they wiped my butt until I was able to!

But my math tutor also has. I was really struggling with math at the beginning of this year. Sixth grade was really easy, and then, I started getting pre-AP. I was really struggling with math. Well, my idea of struggling is having an 83 percent in pre-AP math. That might not be an idea of struggling for someone else, but I really wasn't doing well. I was not making very good grades. I got a math student who's in high school to tutor me. She really helped me with everything, and she explained things really well. I went from around an 85, and now I have a 95 in math. On my most recent test, I made a 95 percent. That's really good. It's going to even out my GPA, and I'm really glad. She made such a difference in my life. She's a senior and going to be graduating this year, and I don't think she realizes how much she helped me. I'm really grateful for her helping me with that.

2. In whose life have you made the greatest difference, and what did you do?

I've made a difference, I guess, in a lot of people's lives. I asked around school, and they said, "You inspire me to never stop trying."

I guess I make a difference in a lot of people's lives, but they're little differences, not very big differences. My cousin was struggling in school in seventh grade last year, and he was having a *really* hard time. He was failing most of his classes. He said I really helped him study for that class, and I really motivated him to actually try hard in school. He's doing pretty well in some of his classes that he wasn't doing too well in. He said that I inspired him to actually try in school, because before he was kind of blowing it off. I think he's going to start doing really well now. Right now I'm trying to help him; he's not doing too well in one of his classes. I want to sit down and help him write an essay for extra credit when he has the time That's what I would do if I was in his position. That's what I want to try to do now.

There are some other things I have also done. I was a Girl Scout a few years ago, and I inspired some girls who were really young. They didn't really know what to do. They were Daisies, which is the lowest age group, and I was a cadet. I was in this rank called the P.A., which means that you are basically a counselor and you help all of the younger Girl Scouts at camp. I taught 140 Girl Scouts how to make this really complicated bracelet; it's called a survival bracelet, made out of parachute cords. It's really hard to make. It took my friends and I an hour to figure that out. I was really surprised, but they all had a really good time. The entire two-hour trip home from camp, they were making them in the car! At the end of the process of making the bracelet, we had to burn the tip of the cord with a lighter to make it stick together. At the end of the trip, I was tired and exhausted. When I got my bags out of the trunk, I had about fifty Girl Scouts run up to me and say, "Hannah, can you burn the end of my cords really quick? I just finished this bracelet on the way home!" Some of them had even made five bracelets on the trip home! I was really proud of them.

I've also helped my friends study, and I explain things to my friends. My friends didn't know what to do for this one assignment in Texas History. Texas History is one of my strong points in school, and I was helping them with this Civil War project, and they had no idea what the Civil War was when we started. I'm a Civil War freak; I think it's so interesting. I explained everything to them, and they were really grateful that I sat down with them and took the time.

Whenever I try to help someone, I noticed that if you sit down and give someone the time — it doesn't have to be that long — if you just sit down and give someone the time, it really makes a difference in their life. I've seen my friends and my family members — even my cousin who I helped. I've seen myself give them thirty minutes, and they just excel in something. It completely changes their day, believe it or not!

Sometimes in the hallway, I'll see kids get picked on and I'll help. I don't like being a bystander. I feel like I have to do something about it. There was this kid being bullied on the bus, and I stepped up and told the kids to stop bullying him. I took him up to the front of the bus and talked to him for the rest of the bus drive.

I don't like being a bystander. I've been like that since kindergarten. My friend was getting picked on, and I was told: *In kindergarten you're at the bottom, in fifth grade you're at the top.* Some fifth graders were picking on my friend, and that was a big deal for me to step up in kindergarten. I was the littlest, puny thing, and they were so big to me, but I told them to stop. He still tells stories about that. He always comes up to me at school and says, "Thank you so much, Hannah, for helping me with that! They don't mess with me anymore!"

That's happened multiple times with me in various schools. I'm kind of a confident person when standing up for people. I just don't let people bully other people. Even if they're not my friend, even if they're the most annoying person in school, which has happened to me once. I still stick up for them because no one should be treated like that—no matter who they are, no matter what color their skin is, no matter their personality. I don't think anyone should be treated the way I see some kids treated.

3. What difference would you like to see in the world, and what are you willing to do to contribute to it?

I think, regarding bullying, it's amazing the numbers of kids who commit suicide. I had a guy come talk about that at my school a few years ago. Probably the numbers have quadrupled in size; it's huge what's going on. Kids are just being so mean to one another, and I really want to stop that. I can't imagine it. I don't get picked on very much at my school, but I know some kids really do, and I can tell it really hurts them. I can tell in the hallway by the way they walk and the way they talk about themselves. They think lower of themselves, and they're really not.

Everyone says *world peace,* but war is something I would really like to prevent. One person can't really stop it, but there is so much controversy with all the nations right now. Fighting over religion; that's what you believe in, but you should not count other people down because of that. I have a really good friend that's Muslim, and he's the nicest person ever. I love him so dearly. His mom wears the scarf around her head. She is the nicest lady ever, so sweet, and she's afraid to go out in public and even shop in her little town because she's afraid of what people will think of her. She shouldn't have to worry about that. They're the nicest people ever, and people think poorly of them just because of what's happening in Afghanistan and Pakistan. My mom and I will take them around town. For example, we'll go eat dinner with them.

It's a good feeling, knowing that you have friends from a different culture, and you're not afraid to show that. If you just talk to one of them, you find what's interesting about their religion and what they think is not right. It's so amazing to learn about all the different kinds of things. They get married really young, and she and her husband had an arranged marriage. She was a lucky one; she was so grateful that she has a really good husband that lets her work and lets her have days off. She said that some of her friends were not so fortunate in doing so, and they got mistreated by their husbands. It's amazing to look into that culture.

I would really like to bring a lot of people together for one day or a weekend — a camp or something — and have different people from all over the country just talk about their cultures and religions. I think that would be really cool and would really make a difference in how people think of each other, even if they're from Pakistan or London or France. I think that would be really cool, and people would be able to spread the word. I think that would be one baby step in solving world peace.

Max Markel

Grade: 10

Hobbies: Wrestling, hanging out, watching movies, spending time with friends and family, and I do origami.

What do you do for fun? Go to the movies, sleep a lot, and hang out with friends

Favorite class: English, because it's something I see a lot of potential in, gaining a lot of knowledge for when I go out into the real world.

What would you like to be, or do, once you've completed school? I'd like to continue the stock investing that I've been doing for the last two years. And I'd like to be an entrepreneur as well.

1. Who has made the greatest difference in your life, and what did they do?

The person who's made the greatest difference in my life is my dad. He's made a huge impact on my life by being such an amazing role model for me. He lives with integrity, he helps others all the time, loves his life unconditionally, and is a model of all those qualities for me daily. My dad has taught me to be courageous and to go for my passions.

My dad helped me through a hard time in my life by introducing me to a poem called "Invictus" by William Ernest Henley, which to me represents honor, courage, and bravery and encourages me to listen to my heart. This poem helped me through some really tough times when I moved across the country.

Here is the poem, "Invictus":

> Out of the night that covers me,
> > black as the pit from pole to pole.
> I thank whatever gods may be
> > for my unconquerable soul.
>
> In the fell clutch of circumstance,
> > I have not winced nor cried aloud.
> Under the bludgeonings of chance,
> > my head is bloody, but unbowed.
>
> Beyond this place of wrath and tears,
> > looms but the horror of the shade.
> And yet the menace of the years
> > finds and shall find me unafraid.
>
> It matters not how strait the gate,
> > how charged with punishments the scroll.
> I am the master of my fate,
> > I am the captain of my soul.

2. In whose life have you made the greatest difference, and what did you do?

I interviewed a few people with this question and my favorite answers came from my mother. She had a really long list of ways I have impacted her life, and I have to admit I was really surprised. I thought I was just her kid. I didn't realize I had made a difference in her life.

I was born deaf in one ear, which, as my mother shared with me, taught her patience. It encouraged her to learn new ways of doing things and gave her a challenge that taught her how to step out of her comfort zone as a mother and as a person. When I was growing up, she had to adapt. She learned sign language, didn't judge me or treat me like I was handicapped in any way, and she had to be patient not only with me but with herself. She was accepting and didn't worry about what other people thought about me or us. The situation challenged her to grow and she did.

I have also impacted my dad just by being by his side throughout his journey in life. I think that his number one value in life is his family, and I'm honored to be a part of that. He is constantly sharing with me how inspirational he thinks I am. I go to the seminars that he teaches, and I participate in the processes at my 100 percent. He really sees me and often tells me that I'm an inspiration to him and others. It's wonderful to have a dad who gives me this type of validation.

3. What difference would you like to see in the world, and what are you willing to do to contribute to it?

There is so much I want to do to make this world a better place. There are two really big ones that come to mind right now.

First, I really want to see the end to homelessness in my lifetime. I've already started an organization called Social Sponsors to help fund the homeless, put the money to good use, and help them in any way we can. That's my first step in trying to do something about this serious problem that I've been passionate about. Ever since I was a little kid and saw people living on the streets, all I wanted to do was to help.

The second one is I really want to see more teens find their passions and gain confidence at a younger age. And I'd like to teach them how important it is to love their life and themselves unconditionally through a personal development environment. I'd like to be not only the trainer for that course, but to teach them by being a model of these qualities myself.

One thing I'd like to teach them is how to take control of their financial life at a young age. I've been trading stocks for a few years now, and I've already been teaching adults how to do it. It's been really great teaching adults and maybe teens would be open to learning it as well. I think I can take these really amazing techniques I've learned and developed and teach them to teens. I started when I was thirteen years old, and I've been very successful at it. I want other teens to be successful at it as well.

Meesha Salaria

Grade: 4

Hobbies: Creating raw food recipes, love writing, enjoy playing board games, look forward to painting, reading, haiku poetry

What do you do for fun? I get fun in riding my bicycle, designing clothes for Barbies, nature photography, and making short films.

Favorite class: Painting, Classical Dancing, and Stephanie Alexander Cooking program at school

What would you like to be, or do, once you've completed school? I am a public speaker, writer, and an author, and I would like to continue to do the same.

1. Who has made the greatest difference in your life, and what did they do?

A lot of people have—from my parents, to my teachers, to my sister. Good people, and not-so-good people. But if you told me to say the first person that comes to mind, it's my mom.

What has my mom done for me? I'll give you an example: She loves and nurtures me. She spends quality time with me. She brings me up whenever I need to have some love, and I need her energy. She has taught me the biggest lesson of my life: *Make do.* So, if I was writing a card to you, and I would write: *Thank you,* but I had a few spelling mistakes in there, she would teach me just how to fix it and add some flowers and butterflies. She'll make it look like a thank you card, and a very pretty one.

She teaches me. If I go to her and say, "Do you like my painting?" she won't ever do anything to impress me.

She'll always say, "Well, I think you could add this to it, and maybe that will make it look a little prettier."

She'll give me the answer and have me fix it. Whenever you have a problem, you do want to have an answer and how you think you can fix it. That makes it easier for you to fix the problem. I love my mom's creativeness.

Did you know that I do not have a TV, a microwave, an iron, or a lawn mower? You may think I live in a jungle; well, we don't. I sometimes watch TV at my grandma's house (for maybe ten minutes), and some of the things are very sad. When I come home I feel a little bit sad. Not having a TV just brings me up in so many ways; some things are really sad, and you just keep thinking about them.

Mom teaches me by example. She does a gratitude jour nal, which is a journal where she writes everything she's grateful for. I used to watch her all the time when I was little, and I started writing my own gratitude journal. The best thing about the gratitude journal is, if you say: *I am grateful for the beautiful colors on a butterfly,* it actually comes in a day; it's happened to me quite a bit! I'll see butterflies fly around with these beautiful colors, and I'm more grateful because I wrote it in my gratitude journal and I'm able to see it. She does that, she inspires me, and she tells me how to handle situations. At school, if I've had a situation and I really need help, I'll go to my mom and I'll say, "Mom, how do I fix this situation?" She helps me with my homework when I need help, and she gives me unconditional love.

The biggest lesson she has taught me is to make do. I'll give you another example. At school lately, we've been using iPads. We usually listen to music on a Friday; I had no music because I recently got mine, and mine is very new. I just thought: *What can I do?* Then—*Bing!*— my mom's idea had come to mind. I was so happy! I went to the iTunes store, and you can usually listen to a couple of the lines of one song; that way you know if you like the song or you don't. All the kids were listening to one song, and in that one song's time, I was able to listen to five or six or seven of them, and it was so much fun! It was two different experiences—when you hear the whole song, it's a different one, and when you hear a little snippet of the song, it's a different experience.

Her *make do* lesson has really helped me in my life. So, who has made the greatest difference in my life? My mom has.

2. In whose life have you made the greatest difference, and what did you do?

I only am a little kid, but my mommy tells me that I have made the greatest difference in her life. Just recently, she had fallen; she slipped while she was coming out of the shower. She crushed her whole cheek frame. Imagine that—that has got to hurt! She had to have it operated on, and they had to put three titanium metal plates in her cheek.

I was very upset, and I said, "I want to be responsible. I'm not going to let my mommy down. I'm going to run the house just like she would." So I did! My dad would pick me up from school, bring my sister and me home, and we would make our lunches for the next day. As a family, we would cook for her. When she used to wake up in the morning, she would never, ever hear us; it was so quiet she used to fall back asleep. I did my own home-work, and I would take it to school. I used every minute I had, and I spent as much time as I could with my mom. I would go to her any time, even when I had situations at school; when she had her fall, I would still go to her and I would hug her. She would always be open for me and my sister. She would always let us come, and she would give me warm hugs and kisses. It's a bit of a complete cycle; she has made a difference in my life, and I have made mine in hers!

3. What difference would you like to see in the world, and what are you willing to do to contribute to it?

I would love to see a healthy world—healthy people, happy people. I would like to see more organic food in the world. Even better would be raw food! When I say raw food, you're probably thinking: *What does she mean by raw food?* I mean zucchini pasta; you can usually get a spiralizer, and you put the zucchini in it and just move the handle. It comes out in noodle texture, and you can add a raw tomato sauce. I would like to see more of that. I would like to see more people grow more veggies, and harvest veggies, and cook veggies.

What am I willing to do about it? I am writing a book right now about the life cycle of the tomato; how [to] grow a seed, what climate to put the tomatoes in, how to harvest a tomato plant, recipes for the tomato plant— relishes so you can put them on bread (it's like a jam, but a fruit version).

My mom asked me, "What would you like as a birthday present?"

I said to her, "I want a tomato plant."

I got fifteen different types of tomato plants, and twenty-four altogether. All the time I would just go there, water it, pick one, hold it in my hand, and be grateful, like: *Thank you, God, for the beautiful tomato plant I have in my hand right now. I'm sure it will give my body a lot of good, and it's very blessed for us.*

Healthy world, healthy people, happy people—that's what I'd like to see more of.

Taggert Gile

Grade: 10

Hobbies: Collecting rocks, playing video games, and watching TV

What do you do for fun? Hang with my friends or play video games

Favorite class: History

What would you like to be, or do, once you've completed school? I want to be a chef.

1. Who has made the greatest difference in your life, and what did they do?

That would probably [be] one of my friends. A lot of times, when I was depressed, I would talk to them, and that's how I'd really get over it. I would talk to them, and they would help me out of my depression when I couldn't really think of doing anything else. A lot of times, when I can't [talk] with my mom, I would still do it, knowing I have people there for me more than I know I do.

I've been bullied and picked on, all throughout my school. I didn't used to have friends here at my new school, or at elementary school. But now, knowing that there was somebody there before or after, when I didn't really think anybody was there for me—always being there, even if it was late at night, I could always talk to them. They would never judge me and lend a supporting shoulder if I needed it.

It's easier to make friends when you think you actually *can*, not feeling all alone in the world, and being able to be braver because of it. Even when people feel alone, they're not alone.

2. In whose life have you made the greatest difference, and what did you do?

It would be one of my friends who constantly hears voices in her head. She constantly second-guesses herself. I've spent some nights actually talking her out of suicide. I was pretty much that supportive shoulder for her—always there to talk to her, telling her that everything was going to be okay. She was like me; she had few to very little friends, and it was very hard for her because she constantly thought she was crazy. Her parents didn't really help her, so I was always that one whom she talked to when she needed help. One night, after her boyfriend broke up with her, her parents were saying it was her fault and that she wasn't good enough for him. They didn't help her at all and sent her into a shame spiral that I helped her get out of.

My friends' lives have changed more because they know that I'm always here, but my life is different because I was able to lend that support. I got to be that person that they could trust to talk to. With my friend that always called herself crazy, I told her that I would never call her crazy. Right now, she's back in a mental hospital she's been to about five times, and I'm always trying to help her whenever I can.

I've probably also helped my brother. My dad wasn't really there for us when we were little; he made promises he was never able to keep. I don't know where he lives right now. My brother and I both helped each other. We're always there for each other whenever we need it. Even just having someone there when you need someone to talk to—we're always there. My brother's actually in the Army right now, and I haven't seen him for about a year now. He's also the father to my adorable niece. I made a difference in his life because when he wanted to join the army, he had a hard time telling my mom. I was there for him, saying, "I know, it was hard for me, but I know this is what you want to do."

3. What difference would you like to see in the world, and what are you willing to do to contribute to it?

I would say stopping the bullying of people just because they are gay, bi, or lesbian, or they have Down syndrome. Just because they are different doesn't mean you should pick on them. I'm in two different clubs that work with kids with learning disabilities like ADD, ADHD, and bipolar; that was also what made making friends harder for me. Just making it so people don't pick on other people just because they're different; they're still people. Just because they need someone to pick on, I believe it's not okay and that should change.

Whenever I hear about people picking on someone, I always try to explain to them how it is different. For example, I'm friends with a bunch of kids who have Down syndrome and learning disabilities. Even when I'm upset, they can somehow always put a smile on my face. So, I would explain to others why bullying is wrong and always try to defend somebody who is being picked on, no matter what it's about.

I'm really good at talking. I try to volunteer when I can, and when I do, I always try to pick the one kid that nobody wants to be with or try to choose the thing that nobody wants to do because they're too scared to do it. Even if I'm scared, I'll still try to do it just so that it gets the word out there.

Talking to people, getting the word out there that there are people you can talk to, can help. At my school, there are a bunch of people who have been through depression or almost committing suicide, and letting them know that there are people they can talk to [is important]. There are always going to be those few people who will say, "This shouldn't change. It doesn't matter if I pick on them." People don't know how it actually feels.

If I were to start this, I would try to get a bunch of my friends together and make posters, or just get the message out there that: *There are people here!* I might even have a list of people they could talk to, kind of like a giant support group for if they ever needed anything. I would start this as soon as possible — whenever my friends, or even my teachers, and I can get together, meet, and try to set it up.

Addison Arnold

Age: 18

Hobbies: Writing mostly, making music, skateboarding

What do you do for fun? The same three things: writing, making music, and skateboarding

Current job: I am working at a factory and, I do, I move around a lot but my main title is Snag Grinder. So basically, I just grind pieces of metal with the grinder.

What would you like to be or do, in the future? The main thing would either be some kind of writer or a musician, for sure.

1. Who has made the greatest difference in your life, and what did they do?

I probably have to say my Dad just because he has always taught me to search for wisdom. He is always teaching me things; he is always doing his best to teach me everything that he knows. And we are a lot alike, and he just, out of everybody, I feel like he has probably made the biggest difference in my life.

2. In whose life have you made the greatest difference, and what did you do?

I guess maybe my girlfriend. Mainly, she has told me that I have taught her a lot and helped her with a lot of things. So I think, out of a lot of people, I think I definitely made a big difference in her life—like just ways of thinking and how to improve your mindset and things like that.

3. What difference would you like to see in the world, and what are you willing to do to contribute to it?

I would definitely like to see people more united and using their heads more, not being so controlled by social media and things like that. Like just being free-minded people, thinking on their own. And, I think writing and music and things like that help a lot of stuff like that, which is one of the big reasons I wanted to do that.

Alyssa Hoffmann

Age: 15

Hobbies: I like to dance, that is my main hobby, and I also do pops.

What do you do for fun? I also dance, and I run for fun.

Favorite class: Probably weight flex — it is like gym.

What would you like to be, or do, once you've completed school? I want to be a dance choreographer.

1. Who has made the greatest difference in your life, and what did they do?

Probably my mom because she has taught me how to be a good person and make good influences on other people's lives. And if I have ever made mistakes, she has helped me, like, be the best person that I can be.

2. In whose life have you made the greatest difference, and what did you do?

Probably my best friend, Macy, because I am always there for her, and [if] she ever has problems, I always talk to her and help her get through it.

71

3. What difference would you like to see in the world, and what are you willing to do to contribute to it?

Oh gosh, I would like, I'd say have people be a lot nicer to each other in this world and [have] there not be so much controversy. What I would do, would be probably spread awareness about it. And talk about it.

Ashley Phillips

Age: 19

Hobbies: I like to play ultimate Frisbee and soccer.

What do you do for fun? I like to hang out with friends, watch Netflix, take naps besides doing homework, I guess.

Favorite class: My favorite class would have to be my Lex Youth Development class that I am taking currently this semester. I am just learning about different ways that I can work with children and youth, specifically, and how to better their recreational experiences.

What would you like to be, or do, once you've completed school? That is still up in the air. I am hoping to be a psychiatrist, specifically to work with children who have multiple personalities disorders or bipolar or some of the rare psychological disorders that you do not really see and a lot of people really do not know how to help. I just want to be that kind of person who is their resource so they can also have a good life.

1. Who has made the greatest difference in your life, and what did they do?

I think the person who made the greatest difference in my life would be my mom. She raised us as a single parent and growing up, it was not always the easiest having to only have one parent around. It was because of her that she pushed us in school, pushed me specifically. I struggled a lot with reading and spelling throughout my early years in elementary school, and she would sit down for hours with me and just do flash cards of words and have me read books. I also saw her go to school, college specifically, while I was going through high school and everything. And she was kind of the main reason why I decided to go to college. I applied to eight different colleges, actually, and she took her time out of her day to take me to every single college tour. She drove all the way to Montana so I could see a college that I wanted to go to. She helps with finances, and she is still making that difference in my life by helping me through. If it was not for her, I would not be the same person I am today, getting an education and chasing after my goals. I go to the University of LaCrosse.

2. In whose life have you made the greatest difference, and what did you do?

I think one of the greatest differences I have made was for a specific person who I worked with in swim class. He was about fourteen, maybe, at the time, and he was in my swim class. He was just kind of lost; he was not really quite sure what he wanted to do. He was not doing very good at school, and I could notice his behavioral issues in class. His mom would always talk to me and, like, tell me how she did not know what to do and every-thing. I felt like really being able to work with him and taking time out my day to help and to tutor him in math because I was very good in math. I helped push him in school because I was always around in high school, still, and we went to school together and stuff. I was able to help him, and he actually ended up improving his grades and his score. And because of that, he decided to go into school, into college. And it was just a great experience, and it was something just for me. I knew working with people and helping people through struggles at times was something I was interested in, and that was some-thing that pushed me to go into my major now.

3. What difference would you like to see in the world, and what are you willing to do to contribute to it?

I guess the biggest difference I would like to see in the world is more compassion and understanding for those who may not always have the best access to care, specifi-cally like mental health issues. I am a psychology major, working with specific people who have anxiety, depres-sion, and different disorders, and seeing how that can affect people's lives. I see the stigma behind it and how not everybody really understands. Even though you are not physically hurt, but you could be just as hurt inside as you would be if you were to hurt your arm or break a leg or anything. I think that would be something as [simple as] having more compassion and understanding of people in general.

Christina Phillips

Age: 19

Hobbies: I like to work out a lot, and I enjoy reading. I like to go shopping with my friends.

What do you do for fun? For fun, I like to go to the movies or go to the beach and just spend time with my family.

Favorite class: Right now, my favorite class is probably Spanish because I feel I can learn the most; I can retain the most knowledge.

What would you like to be, or do, once you've completed school? Right now, I think I want to be healthcare administrator and have ties with international business. I am really passionate about the healthcare field, but I took a class in high school and realized that direct patient care was not for me — so like nursing is not exactly suited for me. I have been kind of interested in the business side of it, and I just want to be able to help people.

1. Who has made the greatest difference in your life, and what did they do?

I would have to say either my mom or one of my Spanish teachers has made the greatest difference in my life. My mom has just supported me through all the hard times that we have gone through, and she has inspired me to work really hard and be able to still play hard at the same time. It has instilled the mindset in me that I can do anything that I put my mind to as long as I work hard enough for it. And my Spanish teacher has influenced me to travel the world and observe other cultures and gain appreciation for what I do have, compared to others.

2. In whose life have you made the greatest difference, and what did you do?

I would have to say the greatest difference I have made was one of my friends in middle school had a rough upbringing, and she had tried to commit suicide. Before, like I saw all the earlier signs, and I went to my guidance counselor and told my mom, and she got the help she needed at Rogers.

3. What difference would you like to see in the world, and what are you willing to do to contribute to it?

One difference that I want to see in the world is healthcare more readily accessible to others like third world countries. I am not entirely sure what exactly I want to do to help contribute to that. I am still kind of deciding what I want to do as a career, but I am very passionate in the field that everyone is entitled to have decent healthcare. I would probably want to come up with a cure for cancer worldwide and have it accessible to everyone, and not just the people that have the money to pay for it. I am really enjoying chemistry and biology, but right now, I also like the business aspect. So right now, I am taking classes like Microeconomics and Applied Business Calculus, which is all very interesting. I work in an accounting department right now and have decided I do not like accounting, but I like the business atmosphere thing. I can still picture myself in a hospital helping others, just not directly helping them, but on the other side.

Dominic Hoffman

Age: 18

Hobbies: I like football, lacrosse, business. Basically anything with active working out.

What do you do for fun? I like to hang out with my friends over the weekends. Lacrosse practice and working out.

Favorite class: My favorite class would probably be business.

What would you like to be, or do, once you've completed school? I would probably go to do a four-year business school and get a degree in that. And then potentially do law school and lawyer wise.

1. Who has made the greatest difference in your life, and what did they do?

I probably have to go with my football coach; his name is Coach Young. He was just really influential. He taught me a lot of life lessons. He basically showed us that we can use different things on the field as well as off the field, leadership-wise, discipline-wise, and things like that. It has really helped me just further pursue my life and be a better person.

2. In whose life have you made the greatest difference, and what did you do?

The greatest difference in someone's life would probably have to be just to continue in the trends of sports—just being a leader to the younger kids. I really like to try to help, and if they have any questions, they can come to me. I feel like they really feel safe around me; they can just come to me with anything, and I can help them in that way. So, I feel like that has been something.

3. What difference would you like to see in the world, and what are you willing to do to contribute to it?

Overall, I would like to see everybody treat each other better. You know, with everything that just goes on in life, all different views. I would like everybody to work together. Not say everybody have the same views and everything, but I want everybody to be able to contribute differently and solve problems together. I would like to be seeing other people potentially doing those things—showing how no matter how the person acts, I can still be nice to them, I can still share my views. I do not have to get mad when somebody contradicts what I say. And things like that. Basically, I would just like to be a role model for people around me so that they can see that and potentially help their lives.

Kobe Patterson

Age: 15

Hobbies: Playing video games, coding, sometimes cooking

What do you do for fun? I usually just sit around and play video games.

Favorite class: Physical Science

What would you like to be, or do, once you've completed school? A video game developer

1. Who has made the greatest difference in your life, and what did they do?

My mom. She has been supporting me for a very long time, literally my whole life, actually. One example is I ended up becoming extremely ill in the past, and no doctors were able to heal me because they were unable to find the cause of my disease. She was able to go, and she was able to create her own care for me.

2. In whose life have you made the greatest difference, and what did you do?

I mostly have to say my brother Rakim because I ended up encouraging him to actually go back to school and graduate. That allowed him to have many more job openings. He was finally able to get a job and move on with his life. If I had not encouraged him to do that, he would probably be in a much worse situation than he is now. He went back to school, and he earned his diploma.

3. What difference would you like to see in the world, and what are you willing to do to contribute to it?

The biggest difference I would really like to see is a change in the climate and people working towards conserving our planet and keeping it from dying because right now the carbon footprint in every country is becoming extremely bad. The world is starting to die, the doomsday clock is close to reaching noon. I would really like for the world — everyone in the world — to come together to try to help save our dying planet. I would be willing to do things like switching to an electric car, possibly, and recycling so I am avoiding throwing waste all over the place. Also, I would try to cut down my usage of electronics, get a Forward panel, and avoid causing more fossil fuels to be released.

Mia Uribe

Age: 14

Hobbies: I like to draw and paint.

What do you do for fun? I play sports, volleyball, and soccer.

Favorite class: Math

What would you like to be, or do, once you've completed school? I would like to be a lawyer.

1. Who has made the greatest difference in your life, and what did they do?

My dad because he is always like giving me, honestly, really great advice, and he helps me get through a lot of things. He really helps me out.

2. In whose life have you made the greatest difference, and what did you do?

I made a difference to one of my friends when I gave her advice that my dad had once given me. She was telling me how she had anger issues, and she was depressed.

And she was just telling me all those things. I helped her out by listening and telling her that she needs to control her issues.

3. What difference would you like to see in the world, and what are you willing to do to contribute to it?

I would like people to not judge each other. I am going into high school next year, and I am not going to judge anyone. I hope no one judges me because I am not coming from where everyone is coming from. Most people that are going to the high school went to the elementary school there, and I did not. So hopefully, they do not judge me. And I know some people will be coming from other areas. I won't judge them.

Mohamad Alabbas

Age: 14

Hobbies: I like to play soccer and basketball.

What do you do for fun? Playing video games

Favorite class: Do I have to pick one, can I pick two? Science and math.

What would you like to be, or do, once you've completed school? I want to be a pilot.

1. Who has made the greatest difference in your life, and what did they do?

My ESL (English as a Second Language) teacher. She always tells me to be my best, and if someone makes fun of my English, say that I'm still learning. The teacher always inspires me to keep going, and when I fail, she encourages me to just try again.

2. In whose life have you made the greatest difference, and what did you do?

My dad and my mom. When my grades weren't very good, they asked me to change them. I did the work, my grades are now up, and they are proud of me.

3. What difference would you like to see in the world, and what are you willing to do to contribute to it?

There is a lot of smoke that comes from cars, and the smoke isn't good for the earth or for us to breathe. I want to make a car [that] runs on something that does not do harm to the planet or the people.

Nevaeh Ebert

Age: 12

Hobbies: Drawing and painting

What do you do for fun? Just dance

Favorite class: Band

What would you like to be, or do, once you've completed school? Artist

1. Who has made the greatest difference in your life, and what did they do?

My mom, because she is always there for me.

2. In whose life have you made the greatest difference, and what did you do?

I made a difference in my family's life because I am always there for them, no matter what.

3. What difference would you like to see in the world, and what are you willing to do to contribute to it?

I'd like to see peace in the world. The best way I can contribute is to do my best to always be nice to others.

Nicole Adams

Age: 18

Hobbies: Dance, working out, and hanging out with friends

What do you do for fun? Probably the same three things

Favorite class: History

What would you like to be, or do, once you've completed school? I would like to be an optometrist and own my own practice.

1. Who has made the greatest difference in your life, and what did they do?

My mom has made the greatest difference in my life because when I was younger she noticed I was having trouble with reading and writing in fourth and fifth grade. One of my teachers was very confused and sent me to the reading specialist in my school. She knew there was something wrong and went and had me tested for dyslexia, which ended up impacting my life greatly. From there, I was able to get special tutoring for my dyslexia and make it so I am able to be at the same level as students without this learning disability. I was able to learn how to rework how my mind works, to feel comfortable.

2. In whose life have you made the greatest difference, and what did you do?

I was a student mentor at after school activities for middle school kids who come and do art. I volunteered there for two and a half years and was able to form very close relationships with these students. It was a place kids who were less fortunate could go to. They were so economically disadvantaged. This allowed me to have a different way to look at life and understand them while they also had a strong role model in their life, someone to look up to because I was slightly older [than] them but still not the age of their parents.

3. What difference would you like to see in the world, and what are you willing to do to contribute to it?

I would like to be an optometrist, open a vision clinic in Haiti, and at this vision clinic, provide eye care and glasses to those in that country. I have very poor eyesight, so I understand the need to be able to have eye care. While there, I also would like to help with their English. Because of my dyslexia, I see the need to have good basic skills like that.

Rachel Krivitz

Age: 12

Hobbies: I like to make art and paint. I like to play music on the flute and piano.

What do you do for fun? I like to do art and hang out with my friends. And play volleyball.

Favorite class: My favorite class is reading.

What would you like to be, or do, once you've completed school? I want to be an equine veterinarian, which is a doctor for large animals. I am passionate about horses and large animals. I would like to help them.

1. Who has made the greatest difference in your life, and what did they do?

My mom has made the greatest influence in my life because she supports me in the activities and decisions that I do and make. I play volleyball, art, music, tennis. She pushes me to do my best. She is a hard worker and influences me to be a hard worker.

2. In whose life have you made the greatest difference, and what did you do?

I influence my friend Gaby. When she has a bad day, I draw her a picture to cheer her up. She loves my art. Just being there and having fun influences her to be happy. I have impacted her life by doing that.

3. What difference would you like to see in the world, and what are you willing to do to contribute to it?

A lot of horses and farm animals are abused in farms for competition, so I want them to stop abusing the animals and to contribute to that. I want to be a vet for large animals, for farm animals, to save families and loved ones.

Safanah Alabbas

Age: 16

Hobbies: I like to play tennis

What do you do for fun? Sometimes I stay after school, stay with a friend, and go off with them.

Favorite class: English class and Math.

What would you like to be, or do, once you've completed school? I would like to be a nurse.

1. Who has made the greatest difference in your life, and what did they do?

My friends. Because when I first came to America, they helped me a lot.

2. In whose life have you made the greatest difference, and what did you do?

I had a friend in school who was sad one day. I asked her why, and she said she was sad because of how people were acting toward her and talking to her. I told her I could understand because the same happened to me.

I told her good things about her, and it made her feel better.

3. What difference would you like to see in the world, and what are you willing to do to contribute to it?

I like to see people change the way they act toward others, especially people whose skin isn't the same color as theirs. Some people are racist because of the skin color or the religion others choose. I think the best thing I can do to make a difference is to stop thinking about how we're all different and see that we all are the same. And, maybe if I change, it will help someone else see this too.

Sireem Alabbas

Age: 12

Hobbies: Volleyball

What do you do for fun? Play video games

Favorite class: Math

What would you like to be, or do, once you've completed school? Be a famous Tik-Tokker. It is an app that is, like, physically tough.

1. Who has made the greatest difference in your life, and what did they do?

My mom and my dad. They taught me everything.

2. In whose life have you made the greatest difference, and what did you do?

Nobody. I will maybe teach them a new language. Help my friends when they speak Arabic; they don't [speak] English. I could speak Arabic, then English to the teachers for them, you know.

3. What difference would you like to see in the world, and what are you willing to do to contribute to it?

To end the fights in the world, to end the fighting. I am sorry, but I can't do anything to change that. Make the world *one peace* together.

Iyonna Bynum

Age: 19

Hobbies: Taking pictures is one of my favorite things to do.

What do you do for fun? I like to try and experience new things. And, I like to hang out with my friends.

Favorite class: I like both math and science.

What would you like to be, or do, once you've completed school? I would like to be successful in the sense of being generally happy in whatever I do. Maybe modeling or serving in the air force as a fusion analyst.

1. Who has made the greatest difference in your life, and what did they do?

My mom has made the greatest difference in my life because she supports me. As I've gotten older, she's let me be more of myself without being restricted. She's always on my side, and whatever struggles I have, she always seems to fix them. Without her, I literally wouldn't be here at all. I have so much to learn from her, and it's so amazing all that she's taught me over the years.

2. In whose life have you made the greatest difference, and what did you do?

One of the people I interviewed and asked how I made a difference in their life was my aunt. She gave me her answer in writing, and this is what she wrote:

> *Iyonna has made a great impact on my life. First, being an aunt to a baby girl and watching her grow into an adult. Me, needing her as much as she needed me. I like to say that I have molded her in some form or fashion. She has taught me, however, how to be a role model and live the straight and narrow. She has taught me how never to give up and keep pushing. Because when no one else was being positive in her sight, I had to keep plugging her with the good stuff she can become. She is a responsible, smart, resourceful, innovator, a motivator, a go-getter, and someone who reaches for every star in the sky. The impact that Iyonna has made on my life can never have a price. [All] I ever wanted was for all I have given to and for her to help her lead with grace, dignity, and confidence!*

Honestly, I have to say that reading this almost made me shed a tear. What she said really means a lot to me because sometimes I can feel unappreciated. She literally watched me grow up, and she's been with me through everything. It was really refreshing to read. It also made my day because I had the biggest grin on my face for the rest of the day. Not even the tornado warnings that were going on at the time could wipe the smile off my face!

3. What difference would you like to see in the world, and what are you willing to do to contribute to it?

I would like the world to be happy. Too many people are mad about things that don't really matter, and they focus on things that are irrelevant. Everyone needs to realize that we are here together, and the goal is to be harmonious. I would like to see a change in people, but I know it would be a hard task. I'm very good at bringing positive energy and making new friends. I can make a difference to one new friend at a time. I can also reach out to people, ask them how they are doing, and truly listen to their answers. People sharing their stories and connecting with me could help me, and together we can accomplish more than we could by ourselves. My first step is to start reaching out to more people to support them, and I've already started.

Advocates

Jackie Van De Walle

Biography

Jackie Van De Walle is a third-generation native San Antonian whose family was involved in farming and ranching at Van De Walle Farms, Inc. She is past president of Van De Walle Industries, Inc.

She was the first female president of the South Texas Farm and Ranch Club, is a past 4-H member, and received the highest honor for a former member, the 4-H Alumni Award.

In June, 2012, Jackie was named "Lifetime Assistant Vice President" of the San Antonio Stock Show & Rodeo after serving seven years as an assistant vice president; leads the Speaker's Committee; is a member of the SALE Leadership Team; a member of the Board of Directors; past Chairman of the Ambassadors Committee for twenty-two years; a member of the Auction Committee and Top Buyer; and a past member of the Souvenir Committee, Cowboy Church, as well as numerous other committees.

YOU Make a Difference

On January 10, 2013, Jackie Van De Walle was induct-
ed into the San Antonio Stock Show & Rodeo's Hall of
Fame along with Richard "Tres" Kleberg and Danny R.
Adams.

On January 30, 2013, Jackie Van De Walle was presented
with the United States Department of the Army's Com-
manders Award for Public Service and the U. S. Army
North (5th Army) and Fort Sam Houston's Commanding
General Coin (Lt. Gen. William B. Caldwell).

Jackie serves as president of the Bexar County Leadership
Advisory Board of the Texas A&M University System's
Texas AgriLife Extension Service. She also serves as one
of seven members of the state-wide Texas Urban Advisory Board, a board that represents the largest urban
counties (covering over 50 percent of the total state population) for the Texas A&M University System and the
Texas AgriLife Extension Service.

Jackie is an advisory board member of the Bexar County Equine-Assisted Therapy Center, Inc. at the Cyndi
Taylor Krier Detention Center. This 501(c)(3) non-profit
educates incarcerated teens with a high school curriculum and provides an opportunity to attain an associate
degree in Equine Science.

Currently, Jackie is serving as an Advocate for One in
Five Minds to raise awareness and end the stigma of
mental illness and increase access to treatment for children whether or not their families can afford it. Services
are provided at the Clarity Child Guidance Center lo-

cated in the Medical Center and at a new clinic located in Westover Hills Medical Park, making both centers available to children and families needing mental health services more accessible.

Note: The *1in5 Minds* represents the national average number of children who struggle with mental illness. Studies show many more go undiagnosed. Please like their page on Facebook (1in5minds.org).

Jackie has served as an advisory board member for the Texas Department of Agriculture District Six, which covers thirty-one counties, including Bexar County.

She is a graduate of the Texas AgriFood master's program through the Texas A&M AgriLife Extension Service, which is dedicated to the expansion of agrifood education to urban and rural areas.

Jackie Van De Walle was awarded the 1998 National Society of Fund-Raising Executives' "Outstanding Volunteer Fund Raiser."

She was inducted into the San Antonio Women's Hall of Fame in 1988 in the category of ranching and agriculture.

She served fifteen years as the chairman of the board of the Alamo Community College District Foundation, Inc., which raises monies for scholarships for the 100,000 students (75,000 full-time and 25,000 part-time) of the Alamo colleges.

She in an alumni and past trustee on the board of trustees of Our Lady of the Lake University, having served for the past nine years (the maximum length of time).

She is former president of Miss Rodeo Texas Pageant, Inc. and was state coordinator for Miss Rodeo Louisiana.

She has worked in many areas of the San Antonio Greater Chamber and other civic organizations throughout the community.

She was the spokesperson for the San Antonio Stock Show & Rodeo in the campaign with the San Antonio Spurs for the new SBC Arena—*Saddles and Spurs*. The name of this arena was changed to the AT&T Center on January 12, 2006.

She also was a community spokesperson for extension of the visitor tax to raise $415 million for improvements for the San Antonio River Walk, amateur sports facilities, performing arts, improvements to the rodeo grounds and Freeman Coliseum, and future AT&T Center upgrades. This measure was passed by voters on May 10, 2008.

Jackie served on the Citizens Bond Committee for the Alamo Community College District. They examined the capital improvement projects for the district campuses across the community due to the rapid growth and enrollment at ACCD. This $450 million bond was approved by Bexar County voters in November 2005. Construction projects have been completed under budget.

On March 23, 2007, Jackie received the "Community Award" at the Outstanding Women of Action gala
awards ceremony.

**1. Who has made the greatest difference in your life,
and what did they do?**

That's an easy one. I consider myself a very blessed person. I was born into a family with strong core values,
good work ethics, and a belief in discipline. They also
instilled my self-confidence but balanced it with humili-
ty. My grandparents and parents both were examples of
community service within our local area with churches
and were always helping others in any way that they
could—not always financially, but spiritually and mentally as well.

They did bring people up to believe in themselves, and I
think that's an admirable quality. They taught me during
their lifetimes we all need to respect and help others. My
grandmother always said—you've heard it before—*To
whom much is given, much is expected.* That's the phrase
that we all hear, but they actually did believe in that.

My daddy always said, "As long as you're able to stand
up, then your job is to reach back down and help somebody else up."

That was kind of obvious in my home. They were
involved; I was born into it. My life became about ded-
icating myself to helping others because of the leading
examples they were.

2. In whose life have you made the greatest difference, and what did you do?

My love and special interest in helping people, especially children, is through education. I think they are the strength that guides my life. I volunteer in many non-profits and educational institutions to provide opportunities for youths to improve themselves through education and a belief that somebody really cares for them. I think that's sometimes missing today. Often, people are being left out while others are selfish, and it comes across differently. When people know you believe and have faith in them, even if you don't really know them, I think they become more inspired.

My grandfather was one of the operators of the San Antonio Stock Show and Rodeo, and I'm a farmer's daughter. I was blessed to do that and be involved with rodeo. Effective leadership. I've been involved on boards; I'm lifetime assistant vice president now. But when you think about rodeo, it's people with the biggest hearts that give their time, talent, and treasure to support a mission of promoting agriculture in education to develop and protect it. So that kind of fits into what I do.

I've served on Our Lady of the Lake University board of trustees, which is where I went to school, and I did that for the maximum term (nine years). It's really difficult to say no to any nuns, so it was really a beginning there. I also chair the Alamo Colleges Foundation that serves the Alamo colleges here in San Antonio. It's five community colleges, and we serve nearly 100,000 full-time and part-time students. This provides scholarships, opportunities for these people who would never have the chance to go to college. Even with programs, it's still difficult and a challenge, so this is a rewarding field.

Presently I'm on a faith advisory board out of Texas A&M University—Houston, Texas—AgriLife Extension Services. This is a board of seven people across the state because the seven large counties in Texas comprise over 50 percent of the population of Texas. What we do is provide education and information on various programs that educate the community and the underserved: nutrition, clothing, food safety, a lot of different dynamics. I'm also president of the Bear County Leadership Advisory Board—part of the Texas A&M AgriLife Extension Services here. We evaluate programs and listen to constituents in the community. We represent the community to improve what is needed for children, adults, seniors, and everyone else in the community.

I'm an advisory board member of the Bexar County Equine assistive therapy program, and that's at the Cyndi Taylor Krier Juvenile Detention Center. I know that sounds strange, but this is a non-profit that helps educate teens who are incarcerated so they can complete a high school curriculum. We also provide an opportunity to obtain an associate degree in Equine Science. I'll tell you what that is. We have a program that uses horses to reach those students because they're shut down: by society, from mental stress, involvement in gangs, problems in life, and many times no family life. They use horses because horses can sense and know there's trust. Using the horses really helps the kids open up mentally, so it's really a good program. Then they don't come out of prison uneducated.

I'm very honored to be an advocate for *One in Five Minds*. The program helps raise awareness and end the stigma of mental illness that kids get today and increases the treatment for these kids, because a lot of these families cannot pay for it. We have a brand-new center in town (San Antonio), and I'm glad to see it's in the neighborhood, off Highway 151. There's lots of people in that new growth area, and this provides good access. Otherwise, we'd only have the wonderful people in the medical center. *One in Five Minds* is the national average for children who struggle with mental illness, but studies show a lot more go undiagnosed.

We hear the stories of kids with cancer, and everybody wants to help. Tell someone your child's struggling with depression, anxiety, or has a mental challenge, and people will blame parents, teachers, society, or anyone, not realizing there's something at the root of that. It takes professionals to find the problems and help the kids themselves and help their families cope. Imagine how hard it is when you can't see anything physically wrong with your child, but you know there is something wrong with them. The therapy helps them and helps their families. I think that's really noteworthy.

You hear people say: *You can't fix what is not broken.*

I'm saying: *You can't fix what you don't see.*

It might be a challenge, but the struggle of that definition, *broken,* is real. It takes groups of doctors and psychiatrists who come and change thinking, helping children find it within themselves. We all see ourselves every day with our problems, and we think that we have issues, but there are so many children. They are innocent, and they don't understand what's happening. It's really a great avenue to have these placement centers, and clarity is one prime example of what we can do to help these kids.

I've done a lot of other things and non-profits, but it's really not about me. I'm just following what my grand-parents taught, my parents taught, and I think every one of us has a commitment when we're born to look out for someone else. I think that's what our mission should be.

3. What difference would you like to see in the world, and what are you willing to do to contribute to it?

Personally, I would like to see the world see *all* issues as relevant, real, and respectable. We get to talk about *One in Five Minds,* and even the kids incarcerated; you don't see what they're really going through. People don't see it as relevant because it's not an outward thing. They might see the effects of the child having a behavioral issue, but it's more than that. They don't see the par-ents who struggle with the misery of watching a child and hoping they can find someone, and finding, finally, someone that can help resolve the issue.

I guess if we all worked collaboratively, changes would occur on many issues and make the world a better place. There's so much good in this world; we need to take a moment and look for it, so that everyone has an improved life. I'll continue to help children until their lives can be as good as mine, because mine was a blessing.

I'd like to see civility. Today, you see road rage, and you see people with bad manners and bad language. I would hope that people would have and encourage better manners and conduct. I think it shows that we're a civil society, we're educated, and those that don't know, need to know. They probably forgot—we respect each other.

I think we need to adopt real strong core values: integrity, really caring, and doing the best we can, even if it's not the top grade. Do what we can to make a difference. Lead by example; that's what I witnessed and I try to do myself. One key issue I always hope to do is keep a positive attitude.

When I was a kid, I'd say, "Daddy, I want new shoes."

He'd say, "Do you *want* new shoes, or do you *need* new shoes?"

I'd have to think about it, and then he'd say, "Before you answer, I want you to think about the man with no feet."

So as you can see, that perspective grounds you by realizing what you really want and need, which are not as important as actually improving a lifestyle with simple things: being able to live happily, not in anguish, and not struggling with anything. Also, I choose to be grateful for people I know, the people I meet, and those I don't meet, whom I could have helped a little bit by being involved in this community. I think that's important.

"Jesse" James Leija

Biography

A gentleman boxer, James Leija is a conundrum in almost all things in life. Choosing a sport with a *take while you can* lifestyle, James Leija refused the mentality then — and now. He gave his mind and body to boxing while he competed and continues to give to those around him in his retirement from the sport.

Most exceptional boxers were raised in the sport and are punching and competing from a very young age. Although James Leija was raised in a boxing family, he did not begin to box until he was nineteen years old. The head start for others did not turn out to be such a big advantage for Leija's opponents. During his three-year amateur career, he racked up a 25 — 5 record and earned his way into the 1988 Olympic Trials. Leija's short amateur career didn't seem to hinder his professional one as he went on to box professionally for over sixteen years, which is almost unheard-of for a fighter of his caliber.

Most professional fighters will take on a nickname meant to promote their own boxing skills and style. On becoming a professional, Leija took the name, *Jesse,* to honor someone else instead of himself: his father Jesse Leija, who trained him.

"Jesse" James Leija's first professional fight came on October 2, 1988, when he beat Oscar Davis in a first-round knockout at the age of twenty-two. Leija went on to be undefeated in his first thirty bouts with 28 wins and 2 draws on his way to his first world championship, the WBC Featherweight title. His final record stands at 47 wins, 7 losses and 2 draws.

During his career, Leija had many accomplishments, including winning two world titles: the WBC Featherweight and the IBA Lightweight. He also fought and defeated fifteen world-rated fighters, three Olympians, and four world champions. While most fighters will seek to *stretch* a career by fighting opponents with lesser-known talents, Leija sought out and fought elite fighters in multiple divisions, including Micky Ward, Azumah Nelson, Gabe Ruelas, Kostya Tszyu, Shane Mosley, and Oscar De La Hoya. In a ploy to *go out on top,* fighters will often select a much weaker opponent to fight in their last bout. James once again proved why he wasn't your average fighter by accepting a fight for the WBC Light Welterweight title against World Champion Arturo Gatti for his final bow.

Leija's bouts were held in some of the most well-known boxing venues, including the MGM Grand and the Mandalay Bay in Las Vegas, Caesar's and the Boardwalk Hall in Atlantic City, Madison Square Garden in New

York City, and the Telstra Superdome in Melbourne, Australia. With all that travel, Leija never forgot where his home was and hosted twenty-two bouts in San Antonio, one being a *first event* in the new Alamodome.

With the kind of success James Leija experienced in the ring, he could have easily dropped out of sight and into retirement, never looking back. Instead, Leija not only looked back, but he turned around to pull up the less fortunate. Knowing the benefit of sports and competition, Leija set out to help those who may never have had a chance to play sports by backing the Miracle League of San Antonio. The league is an organization that provides children with mental and/or physical challenges an opportunity to play baseball as a team member in an organized league. Leija's support for the league is very evident, as he was honored at the 2nd Annual Miracle League All-Star Evening this spring. His Leija Dodgers will once again take to the "Field of Dreams" for the fall 2012 season.

Leija has also joined up with the San Antonio Area Foundation to support the South Texas Hispanic Fund. This outreach fund is aimed at benefiting the local Hispanic community through grants that address issues in education, health and human services, community development, and arts and culture. It is not a coincidence that the fund is supported and spotlighted through its annual Ringside SA boxing gala event.

In retirement from competition, Leija decided to give back to the sport he loves and opened the ChampionFit

Boxing Gym, where he and his team train a wide range of individuals, from teens to mothers, to business professionals alongside amateur and professional boxers. The gym doesn't just focus on boxing technique but provides its members with a guide to an overall healthy lifestyle.

Leija is respected by people in the boxing world, competitors and spectators alike, as well as those in his community. He competed in the ring and now moves in business with integrity, self-discipline, hard work, and tenacity. He has been honored for his success in and out of the ring and was most recently inducted into the San Antonio Sports Hall of Fame.

James Leija's sporting and business accomplishments, alongside his community support, are enough to make him a legend in his town, and neither are his most evident attributes. It is one thing to be admired from afar, but Leija is also loved by those closest to him. The Leija family, as a whole, is a true testament to who James Leija is. The family support Leija receives from his wife and children is enough to show he is a dedicated family man who is loved by those around him.

1. Who has made the greatest difference in your life, and what did they do?

There are several people in my life that have made differences, but I think the ones who made the greatest difference in my life had to have been my parents. My parents—especially my mom—are the ones who have shown me how to love (and how to get back love), how to have respect for everyone, and how to help the needy. When I was young, my mom would always gather our clothes or our toys and give them away to the more needy families here in San Antonio. I did not understand that when I was young, so I would get upset knowing that my mom was giving away our toys, or sometimes our clothes. As I got older, I realized that my mom was giving back to the less fortunate. We weren't even a wealthy family; we were needy ourselves, but my mom always knew that there was someone that needed it more than we did. That's how I learned to always give back in my life. That's why I've always had foundations and work to give back to the kids here in San Antonio and the surrounding area.

I think that my big contribution to San Antonio has been because of my mom and my parents because they always showed me how to love and how to give back.

2. In whose life have you made the greatest difference, and what did you do?

That's a hard question because it's always someone who has been the receiver that's going to be able to answer that question. I've always given back to my community, but who's to say how big I've given back to them?

The people I think I gave to more than anything else are my kids. I have worked hard in my career to make sure my kids get the best education. My wife and I have made sure that our kids have a strong foundation in love and in support so they can always do well outside the home and in the community. I think my wife and I have done so much to give to our kids, but that's the question that my kids would have to answer one day, if that's been their biggest gifts from us.

That's what I've always done; I want to be a father first. I'm a father, a supporter, a husband, and then I'm the boxer second or third. I think that the biggest contribution I want to give to my kids is teaching them how to love: love all, love one, love everyone, and always give back.

3. What difference would you like to see in the world, and what are you willing to do to contribute to it?

There are a few things. One of the things I'd like to see in the world is people respecting themselves more, as far as physically and mentally being stronger about health. One [thing] I'm doing about it is I have my own fitness gyms, and I teach health. I teach people how to get the best out of themselves, and to be strong-willed, strong-bodied, and mentally focused in themselves throughout their lives.

One of the other things, as well, is for everyone to really love one another and to respect one another. There are so many labels in the United States and around the world; there's Catholics, there's Baptists, there's Protestants, there's Christians — there are so many people who put labels on each other — politicians and such. We're all humans, and we should all love each other, love one another because of that, not because of the label we put upon ourselves. If we would just strip all those labels away, we could realize we are all just one. We all have the same blood inside us, all red, and we all need to just love one another, regardless of where we're from, what our last name is, or the color of our skin. If we could strip all those labels away, it would be a better world.

Judge Laura Parker

Biography

Judge Laura Parker, 386th District Court

Judge Parker was appointed to the 386th District Court in September of 1999. She presides over a general jurisdiction court with a preference for juvenile matters. Judge Parker is board certified in juvenile law by the Texas Board of Legal Specialization. In addition to her regular juvenile docket, Judge Parker presides over three specialty courts: a juvenile drug court, a mental health court for girls, and a domestic minor sex trafficking court. In 2011, the governor appointed Judge Parker to serve on the executive board of the Texas Juvenile Justice Department, the state agency overseeing juvenile justice in Texas. She is the chair of the Bexar County Juvenile Board and previously served as the Local Administrative Judge for the Bexar County District Courts.

She is also a frequent lecturer on juvenile law topics. Prior to her appointment to the 386th District Court, Judge Parker served as an assistant district attorney in Bexar County.

She obtained her BA in Hispanic Studies from Vassar College in 1987 and graduated cum laude from St. Mary's University School of Law in 1992. In addition to her judicial duties, Judge Parker serves on the board of directors for Communities in Schools and the ChildSafe Advisory Council and is active with SA 100 and Impact San Antonio. She also served on the Juvenile Law Council of the State Bar of Texas from 2003-2009 and is a Life Fellow of the Texas Bar Foundation.

Note: Since the collection of material for this publication, Judge Parker was appointed to the new Felony Impact Court in San Antonio.

1. Who has made the greatest difference in your life, and what did they do?

I think my father has made the biggest difference in my life. He taught me so much about honesty, integrity, and working hard to help other people. He did a lot of pro-bono work in his career, and I'd seen that as I was growing up: everything from helping environmentalists to helping a Navajo code-talker finally get his benefits from the Veterans Administration. When I decided to become a lawyer, I think it was to practice in his model. Personally and professionally, he has been my biggest influence. After seeing the way he works, and the kind of father and family man he is—taking care of me, my brother, and my mother—it has really taught me a lot about the kind of person I want to be.

2. In whose life have you made the greatest difference, and what did you do?

I hope I've made the greatest difference in the life of my daughter. She is in sixth grade, and I think — through the kind of work that I do, being a juvenile judge — I see so many parents that do have shortcomings or have experiences in their families that derail the positive influence they could be on their own children. I think it's made me take great care in approaching her in a way I feel is going to help her be a successful person and a good person. Hopefully, she'll be able to avoid the kind of trouble that kids who don't have positive influences in their life are unable to avoid for some reason. I'm hoping I'm making the greatest difference for her in a way. It's hard to say; I guess we'll find out when she's grown. She's a very strong person herself, smart and conscientious; I can't take credit for all her good points, but I definitely see through my own work that having a good parental influence and taking very seriously the job of being a parent, I think, leads to successful things happening for your kids.

3. What difference would you like to see in the world, and what are you willing to do to contribute to it?

I think it kind of goes back to my previous answer. What I would like to see is a new generation of parents who have the skills to help their kids be successful. I do see so many kids who aren't successful, and it has a lot to do with their family dynamic and generations of parents who weren't prepared parents. So it's hard to really blame the current parents; I don't know where the societal breakdown happened, but again, it's a generational thing.

What I'm willing to do—and I feel like I am doing—is use my position and my interest in kids to try to make a difference for the kids here in San Antonio. A lot of times, it's one kid at a time, and we're not completely successful. I sort of operate on a starfish theory; I do what I can for the ones I can help and try to not be thrown off track by the ones it doesn't work out for. I've started a project here in Bexar County to assist juveniles with specialty problems—mental health problems, kids who are victims of sexual exploitation—trying to work with them and their families to repair relationships and get people on track as a family so they'll be able to succeed in our society. It takes a lot of time; these kinds of cases take almost all my time. I feel like I have the time to devote to it, and I'm hoping to start more projects. I've been bringing on new projects about every two to three years, and my days are getting filled up.

Then, I also use my position to seek out issues like the *One in Five Minds* campaign and similar causes. I think being a juvenile judge really gives me a platform to talk about important issues and bring awareness about important public issues like these. I think I have to be willing to do it, go out and talk about it, and go above and beyond what courtroom duties require to make that kind of an impact. That's what I'm trying to do— use the position—to get on committees and to speak publicly about issues that are important to kids and use that in that way.

Keb' Mo'

Biography

It all took off for Keb' Mo' in 1994, with the self-titled release under his newly coined Keb' Mo' moniker, and over the years, he has proven that he is a musical force that defies typical genre labels. Album after album, fourteen in total, garnered him four Grammy Awards and a producer/engineer/artist Grammy certificate for his track on the 2001 Country Album of the Year, *Timeless: Hank Williams Tribute*. He has received eleven Grammy nominations in total, including Country Song of the Year for "I Hope," co-written with The Dixie Chicks, and three alone for his 2014 self-produced release, *BLUESAmericana,* including Americana Album of the Year. Keb' has also been awarded eleven Blues Foundation Awards and six BMI Awards for his work in television and film.

Over the past two decades, Keb' has cultivated a reputation as a modern master of American-roots music through the understated excellence of his live and studio performances. Artists who have recorded his songs include: B.B. King, Buddy Guy, the Dixie Chicks, Joe Cocker, Robert Palmer, Tom Jones, Melissa Manchester, Solomon Burke, and the Zac Brown Band, to name a few. The list of artist collaborations comprises a who's who in the music industry and includes: Bonnie Raitt, Taj Mahal, Vince Gill, Amy Grant, Jackson Browne, Natalie Cole, Lyle Lovett, India Arie, James Cotton, Bobby Rush, Timothy B. Schmit, Marcus Miller, and many more. His guitar playing has garnered him two invites to Eric Clapton's acclaimed Crossroads Festival and has inspired leading instrument makers Gibson Brands to issue the *Keb' Mo' Signature Bluesmaster* and *Bluesmaster Royale* acoustic guitars and Martin Guitars to issue the *HD-28KM Keb' Mo' Limited Edition Signature* model.

He has been featured in TV and film, playing Robert Johnson in the 1998 documentary, *Can't You Hear the Wind Howl?*, appearing three times on the television series *Touched By An Angel*, and portraying the ghostly bluesman Possum in John Sayles' 2007 movie, *Honeydripper*. Keb' created "Martha's Theme" for the TV show, *Martha Stewart Living*. Keb' also wrote and performed the theme song for the hit sit-com, *Mike & Molly*, created by Chuck Lorre, and was music composer for TNT's *Memphis Beat*, starring Jason Lee. In early 2017, nine songs from Keb's extensive catalog were featured in the film *Signed, Sealed, Delivered: Higher Ground* on the Hallmark Movies and Mysteries channel. This film was also Keb's first feature film leading role. He appears as Howlin' Wolf in an episode on the CMT series, *Sun Records* and can be heard playing his original song "Operator." Keb' has played his iconic version of "America The Beautiful" in the series finale of Aaron Sorkin's *The West Wing,* as well as at the actual White House for President Obama.

Keb' Mo' has been a long-time supporter of the Playing for Change Foundation (PFCF), a nonprofit organization that creates positive change through music education. PFCF provides free music education to children in nine countries, including Brazil, Bangladesh, Ghana, Mali, Nepal, Rwanda, South Africa, and the United States and has established twelve music schools around the world. They also work with partners to address basic needs in the communities where they teach, including education, clean water, food, medicines, clothing, books, and school supplies.

Additionally, Keb' is a celebrity mentor with the Kennedy Center's Turnaround Arts program, which focuses on elementary and middle schools throughout the U.S. This highly successful program began under the guidance of Michelle Obama and the President Obama's Committee for the Arts and Humanities. Each artist adopts an under-performing school and becomes a mentor — working with teachers, students, parents, and the community to help build a successful arts education program. Keb' enjoys his mentorship at The Johnson School of Excellence in Chicago, Illinois.

In 2017, Keb' Mo' released *TajMo,* a collaborative album with the legendary Taj Mahal. The multi-generational duo went on to tour the U.S. and Europe in support of their album, which has since earned a Grammy Award for best contemporary blues album.

1. Who has made the greatest difference in your life and what did they do?

I believe that every single person makes a difference, and you can't measure who did the most. One may seem larger than the other one, but the smallest things sometimes make the biggest differences.

The person who has made the biggest difference in my life would be my father. He started me in life with one phrase and it's followed me my whole life. Every time my father saw me he'd ask me about this one Bible verse that he taught me: *Seek ye first the kingdom of heaven, and all else will be added.*

Everything in my life became a derivative of that statement. Things like: *Do what you love and the money will follow.* This is what my father taught me.

2. In whose life have you made the greatest difference and what did you do?

I think I've made the greatest difference in my son's life. When he was born, he inspired me to be more. I realized at that time I really didn't have anything I could give him — nothing to share with him — because I hadn't succeeded in life or done anything significant yet.

I know that children do what you do, not what you say, and I realized that my actions were more important than any words I could have told him. I did my best to teach him by example and not by using just words.

Here is a text that was sent to me some time ago by my ex-wife. It was written by my son:

My Dad

My dad is like a blue whale singing.

My dad is like a nice lion, with someone to care for.

My dad is as talented as a dolphin playing the guitar.

My dad is as creative as an artist playing the harmonica.

My dad is like a horse, riding me somewhere I really want to go.

He wrote that when he was very young. When I see him now that he's grown and matured, I see him as a derivative of my father giving me a gift that I can in turn hand down to my son.

3. What difference would you like to see in the world, and what are you willing to do to contribute to it?

The difference I'd like to see most in the world is an overall change in priorities. Pointing our priorities away from money, riches, and what you can get, and focusing more along the lines of people really caring for each other like one cares for their family. I'd like to see people being in community with one another. I know this happens already in some places, but it's not a priority on a national or global scale.

I'd like to see the priority be: *What can you do for your brother? What can you do for other people? How can we raise our children better?*

We should focus our energy on love rather than always being worried and throwing money whenever we have a problem. Why do we need money to help people?

And what would I sacrifice to see this happen? If it meant that I couldn't be who I am, an entertainer, a little bit famous, if I had to give up my *stuff,* if I couldn't play music for thousands of people all the time . . . I'd give that up in a heartbeat to live in a world like I just described. If I had to just work a regular job, I would do it to live in a world where everyone loved and cared for each other. I would give up everything but my life and my health. I would need those things to be able to contribute in the best way possible.

I dream of a world where we don't need a police department, a military, a world where you don't have to worry about someone coming to steal your stuff or trying to kill you for it. I believe we all really should take care of each other in that kind of way, feed each other, not in a way where one can't excel, not in a communistic kind of way where people are forced to be equal, but in a way where everyone is looked after from birth. Every child gets to learn, and we all get to be what we want to be. When one falters, gets mean, and maybe hurts somebody, we all gather around that person and support them. Clearly, they are not getting what they need when they lash out like that, so we put our focus on being there for them and giving them what they need. I heard one time that they do that in African villages. When someone kills somebody, they all gather around that person because it means that the village has failed, not the person who acted out.

It would be great to live in a world we don't have to do a book like this. We don't have to have campaigns to raise money to help groups of people seen as less fortunate. No one is less fortunate; they're just being left behind, left out, or not cared for.

I think we could improve the lives of our people if we put our focus on life, love, and family first, before money, and let money be something that we only use to fuel those three things. This world would be a better place if we put our focus on living a good life, love, and family.

Senator Leticia Van de Putte

Biography

Leticia R. San Miguel Van de Putte (born December 6, 1954) is an American politician from San Antonio, Texas. She represented the 26th District in the Texas Senate from 1999-2015. From 1991 to 1999, Van de Putte was a member of the Texas House of Representatives. In 2014, she was the Democratic nominee for lieutenant governor but lost the general election, 58–38 percent, to her Republican senatorial colleague, Dan Patrick of Houston. Following that defeat, she then resigned from the Texas Senate to run for mayor of San Antonio, which she narrowly lost to Ivy Taylor, 52–48 percent.

Van de Putte was born in Tacoma, Washington, the oldest of five children of Daniel and Isabel San Miguel, a sixth-generation Tejano family. Her father was stationed at Fort Lewis when she was born. The family returned to San Antonio, where she was subsequently reared. Van de Putte has six children and six grandchildren with her husband, Pete.

1. Who has made the greatest difference in your life, and what did they do?

My children have made the greatest difference in my life, and the only thing that they've done is accept and give love! I say that they've made the difference in my life because that's just such a focus and a priority, but it's also a source of intense joy. For me, almost everything I do either starts or begins with my kids, and now my grandkids. I know that when you think who's made a difference in your life, most people say their parents and grandparents. My family—my grandparents and parents—did really influence and shape my life by giving me very, very deep roots and then, at the right time, maybe some very strong wings. As far as the difference about purpose, acceptance, and pure joy, it's been my six children, and now my grandchildren.

2. In whose life have you made the greatest difference, and what did you do?

I think that I have probably made the biggest difference in the lives of the people I've come in contact with because of my work; my work in two realms. Probably all of the public policy as a legislator, and what I've been able to do there, either through the budget, or through laws. The second thing is the people I've come into contact with as a healthcare professional, whether it has been as their neighborhood pharmacist or whether it has been as a healthcare professional on a *code blue* team (helping resuscitate people back to life). It is those people that I have directly touched in some way by my professional actions, and I say *professional* in my job as a legislator and my job as healthcare professional.

3. What difference would you like to see in the world, and what are you willing to do to contribute to it?

I've thought about it a lot, and what difference would there be in the world? I think for me, it's that constant struggle for the common good. People coming together in a collective body, in a collection of either community or maybe even very cohesively in a neighborhood, whatever the common good is. Being that a week ago we celebrated Martin Luther King's birthday, and in San Antonio we have the largest march—not a parade with marching bands and things like that. It's just a walk, and it starts out with a garbage truck. I, and 175,000 of my closest friends, we marched.

There is so much you can read about what Martin Luther King said, but for me, the most powerful is: *The most pressing and persistent question we ask ourselves is: What have we done in the service of others?*

That's really what I think is what I would like to see changed in the world. What is our daily perspective? What have we done in the service of others? Not individual agendas, but what have we done for each other? Whether it is unleashing that creative class of writers, painters, playwrights, and musicians or the new technology gurus that work in the digital world. Whether they are scientists that are pushing the edge, or if it is somebody who is a community activist or organizer. What have we done in service to each other and for others?

If you were to ask me this last year at this time, I might have had very different answers. The reason is life's big events shape you, and last year was a really hard year for us as a family. We lost our infant grandson in May to SIDS; he was almost six months old. It's your worst nightmare when you wake up and the baby doesn't. Then six weeks later, we lost my dad, the patriarch in our family, in a horrific traffic accident. We were still reeling from the baby's death.

This summer, the legislature had a toxic, hostile, special session on reproductive rights, and it was brutal. I had to return during a filibuster, the day my dad died; right when we finished the eulogy in our family, I had to return to the legislature. Then it kept piling up; we had an employee at my husband's business die crossing the street. It was horrible; he was young, he was promising, and he was only twenty-seven years old and had only been with us for about three years. Then a favorite uncle, who was my husband's business partner as well, and in September, my dear mother-in-law, who was the matriarch of my husband's family.

When you lose so much of your roots and your future all in one, then it really puts priorities in focus. For me, I may have told you a year ago that it was some sort of thing that was really idealistic. But when you lose so much of the important members of your family, it really gives you a focus and a priority that I may not have had last year.

I think, in tempering my answers, you've got to figure that my answers may be a little different than others, but when you bury your grandbaby, and then your daddy, and your precious mother-in-law all in the same time frame, it really adds a different perspective. It made me think about what's really important, and for me, that's my kids. They're all grown; they're all out of the house and, thankfully, on someone else's health insurance plan because they're finished in college. They've got jobs, are couples, and they're married and on the way to having families of their own. When you have to face so much personal tragedy, it leaves you with the *whys?* Then you realize you just can't focus on that. You just hold tight to the people that you love.

If there's anything I have learned, it's that you allow people to grieve because there's usually pretty great grief when there's been great love. Particularly for us, there was so much that we lost, and we had to depend on each other. My family is stronger, I think—much stronger, both mentally and with priorities because we had to face it. It's all about making those connections to people, in a very personal way, and realizing how precious everyone is, and how much potential and how much love they're capable of. When you can bring the happiness and share that, it makes it all worthwhile.

Conclusion

We hope you enjoyed reading the book.

Our hope is that, by this point, not only were you inspired by the answers that other people gave, but their answers revealed to you ways in which you may have inspired others or made a difference in their lives. We invite you to jot down anything that has come to mind.

And while you're in this energy, please go to the *One in Five Minds* website (1in5minds.org) and make a donation.

Next, we'd like to share a story with you.

Who You Are Makes a Difference

Before Facebook, the most popular social media site was Myspace. People would build a personal or band page, connect with friends and family, and make new friends from all over the world. Myspace also had groups with specific themes, and I joined a group called Committed to Love. Because my wife and I were relationship experts and were new to coaching, I decided I would go into the Committed to Love group and offer free coaching to anyone who wanted it for the purpose of connection and to hone my relationship coaching skills.

One day, I logged into the group and saw that one of the teens I had met in the group was online. I sent a message saying: *I see you are online. I hope you are having a great day. I want to you know that you have made a difference in my life.*

She replied: *Really, how?*

I told her we are all making a difference whether we know it or not. There were a few things she had shared with me in our chats in the past, and they had touched my heart and made me think of things in a different way. We chatted for another twenty minutes or so and then said our goodbyes.

A few days later, I received the following message from that teenager:

> *I want you to know that you saved my life the other day. I thought that nobody saw me or cared about me. I was feeling depressed and unseen. I had a handful of pills and a glass of water in my hand when you messaged me and told me that I had made a difference in your life. The chat we had pulled me back and talked me out of killing myself. If I have made a difference in your life, maybe I have done the same for others, too, and just don't know it. Thanks for making a difference in mine. Thanks for saving my life.*[1]

This experience led me to become a very successful coach, speaker, and book publisher because making a difference (by helping others to see how they make a difference) has always been my top priority.

---

1 Story written by Keith Leon S. and previously featured in the book, *The Profit of Kindness: How to Influence Others, Establish Trust, and Build Lasting Business Relationships* by Jill Lublin.

We never know how we are touching people's lives. One smile, one hello, one note or letter, one hug can make all the difference in the world.

You make a difference!

Thank you for being who you are and doing what you do. Thank you for supporting young people by reading this book. May your life be filled with the love you deserve.

Keith Leon S.

About *One in Five Minds*

Advocates for Children's Mental Health

The *One in Five Minds* campaign, sponsored by Clarity Child Guidance Center, was created to raise awareness about children's mental illness, to break down stigma, and to increase access to treatment. Many times parents and community members hesitate to speak up or to ask the important questions about mental illness because of stigma. *One in Five Minds'* goal is that no one will be afraid to speak about mental illness and that all children in Bexar County who need treatment will be able to access it.

One in Five Minds strives to educate the community, parents, professionals, and leaders about mental illness. We do so by engaging and educating parents and their support system about mental illness: its reality, its treatment, and its prevention. We publish educational materials on our website, hold learning events open to the public, promote support and learning options in the community, and advocate for causes that help children and families. Mainly, our goal is to provide important information, resources, and a community so that families no longer struggle alone.

Since it was launched in March 2013, *One in Five Minds* has reached thousands of families who have visited our website, heard a presentation, or attended a workshop.

We have hosted nationally recognized guest speakers like Liza Long, Pete Early, Kay Warren, Senator Creigh Deeds, Randi Silverman, Cinda and Linea Johnson.

Most importantly, *One in Five Minds* has helped many parents reach out for help and support for the first time and that's what we're the proudest of.

Key Advocates Include:

- Kimberly Ridgley, EdD, LPC, CSC—Director of Guidance and Counseling, NISD

- Steven R. Pliszka, MD—Chairman, Department of Psychiatry, UT Health

- Jackie Van De Walle—Lifetime Assistant Vice President, San Antonio Stock Show & Rodeo

- Justice Luz Elena D. Chapa—Fourth Court of Appeals Justice

- Deborah Healy, PsyD—Assistant Professor and PsyD Training Director, OLLU

- Leticia Van de Putte—Former Texas State Senator, District 26

- Al Philippus—Vice President of Corporate Services and Security Division, Valero Energy Corporation

- Amparo Ortiz—Media Professional

- Joaquin Castro—Congressman, District 20

- Honorable Laura Parker—Senior District Judge, 386th District Court

- Judge Nelson Wolff—Bexar County Judge

How You Can Help!

If you're reading this, you likely recognize how important it is for children to be understood and get help when needed. Maybe you are a parent or a relative of a child who got support thanks to this campaign.

If you would like other parents to benefit as well, please consider helping us with a donation today. Clarity Child Guidance Center is the nonprofit 501(c)(3) managing *One in Five Minds,* and your donation receipt will come from them.

Donations will be used strictly to help fund the *One in Five Minds* campaign and will fund expenses, such as promotion and event costs, which will allow us to reach and help many more parents who need this information.

We also welcome corporate sponsorships and have a program that gives such donors an opportunity for great exposure in the community.

For more information, please contact Gerard Migeon at Gerard.Migeon@claritycgc.org or call him at 210.582.6467.

www.ingramcontent.com/pod-product-compliance
Lightning Source LLC
Chambersburg PA
CBHW052104090426
42741CB00009B/1670